Pursued

A Study from Genesis to Revelation

Pursued

God's Relentless Love for YOU

JENNIFER COWART

Abingdon Women/Nashville

PURSUED
God's Relentless Love for YOU

ISBN 978-1-5018-7808-4

21 22 23 24 25 26 27 28 29 30 — 10 9 8 7 6 5 4 3 2 1
MANUFACTURED IN THE UNITED STATES OF AMERICA

Dedicated to my Fathers:
my heavenly One and earthly one,
both of whom have pursued me my whole life

Contents

About the Author

Jennifer Cowart is the executive and teaching pastor at Harvest Church in Warner Robins, Georgia, which she and her husband, Jim, began in 2001. With degrees in Christian education, counseling, and business, Jen oversees a wide variety of ministries and enjoys doing life and ministry with others. As a gifted Bible teacher, Jen brings biblical truth to life through humor, authenticity, and everyday application. She is the author of three women's Bible studies (*Pursued*, *Fierce*, and *Messy People*) and several small group studies coauthored with her husband, Jim, including *Grounded in Prayer* and *Living the Five*. They love doing life with their kids, Alyssa, Josh, and Andrew.

Follow Jen:

jimandjennifercowart

jimandjennifer.cowart

Website: jennifercowart.org or
jimandjennifercowart.org
(check here for event dates
and booking information)

Introduction

Hi, friend! Welcome to *Pursued*!

Have you ever been pursued? If it was by law enforcement, a wild animal, or an unwelcome admirer, then I'm guessing it was a pretty bad experience. But if you have ever been pursued by someone who wants nothing but the best for you, then you know what real love is.

Friend, you are pursued by the God of the universe, and this is very good news! We all want to be loved. We long to be desired, pursued—whether by a special someone, our friends, or others in our lives. This longing for love and acceptance is the underlying story of your life and mine, and it's the overarching story we see throughout the Scriptures. Although there are many sub-stories in the Bible, there is really just one main theme: God's relentless love for us! From Genesis to Revelation, we see that God wants us to know Him, to love Him, and to live our lives in relationship with Him.

In *Pursued*, we will explore God's great love for us from Genesis to Revelation. We will see how God passionately pursues people who do not deserve His love, and we are those people! Like Cain, Abraham, Sarah, Rebekah, David, the woman caught in adultery, Peter, and so many others, we are the ones who have broken relationship with God. But He runs after us anyway to bring us home. Together we will study a great love story and discover that it is our story!

This workbook contains six weeks' worth of devotional Bible lessons, with five lessons for each week. I call them devotional lessons because they include both Scripture study as well as reflection and prayer. I hope you will give yourself the gift of time alone with God to savor His Word and allow Him to speak to you. You may want to find a quiet place to do your devotional each day.

Each day the lesson follows the same format:

Settle: As you begin each lesson, I encourage you to just be still for a few moments and allow your heart and mind to settle. In Psalm 46:10, we are told to "be still, and know that I am God!" In the fast-paced world in which most of us operate, being still, breathing deeply, and resting in God's presence can be challenging. So, I encourage you as you begin each day's lesson to give yourself the sweet treasure of settling your heart, mind, and soul in your heavenly Father's presence. This alone can be a life-changer as you go through the study.

Focus: Next, focus your mind on God's Word, reading a thematic verse and a Scripture from the main story for the day. Isaiah 55:10-11 (TLB) has a promise for those who dwell on God's Word:

¹⁰As the rain and snow come down from heaven and stay upon the ground to water the earth, and cause the grain to grow and to produce seed for the farmer and bread for the hungry, ¹¹so also is my word. I send it out, and it always produces fruit. It shall accomplish all I want it to and prosper everywhere I send it.

Reflect: Now it's time to get to the story and think about how it speaks into your life. God's Word is so rich, and the stories of people in the Bible who were pursued by God's reckless and relentless love have so much to teach us. Their personal stories within God's bigger love story are relevant to us today. As you consider these stories, which may be familiar to you, try to look at them with new eyes. Invite God to give you fresh insights to enrich your life. Space is provided for recording your responses and completing exercises.

Pray: Finally, be still once again and enter into a time of prayer, asking the Holy Spirit to speak new truths of love, peace, and wisdom into your life. I will offer either a prayer or a few suggestions each day to help your time with God be fresh and interesting.

As you begin and end each day's lesson, I encourage you to be creative in your approach to connecting with God. He is a creative genius; just look at the giraffe, butterfly, and anteater! Obviously, God likes variety and creativity. So at times, I will encourage you to try some new things in the Settle and Prayer segments of the lessons. For instance, if you're musical, you may want to begin by singing or playing an instrument. If you're artistic, you may want to end each day by sketching or painting. Perhaps your gift is the written word; then journal what God is speaking to you. You also may want to incorporate praise and worship music (I have included a few song suggestions, but feel free to choose your own) as well as dance or stretching and other physical activity into your devotional study time. Be creative! Think outside your usual practices and try something new.

Before you get started, gather all the supplies you'll need: your Bible, this workbook, a pen or pencil, and any items you need for creative expression—such as a journal, a sketch pad, an instrument, or a device and playlist. Have your tools easily accessible so that nothing deters your time. Another trick I've found helpful is to keep a notepad handy so that if your thoughts begin to drift to things you need to do later, you can just jot them down so they don't steal your time with God.

Friends, it took me many years to realize that God was pursuing me. I thought I had to pursue Him in order to find Him. What a relief to know that He was seeking me all along. The personal stories of the characters we will be studying reveal the same thing. God was running after them—just as He's running after you. No matter what you've done or not done, no matter how far you've drifted or how disconnected you've felt, you are loved. In fact, you are pursued!

Blessings, *dear friend,*

Jen

Week 1

Pursued from the Very Beginning

CREATION

Day 1

Settle

Take in a deep breath and release it slowly. Allow your mind to slow down and your thoughts to center on God's goodness and beauty. Even if only for a few minutes, allow the stresses of your day to disappear, and give God your full attention.

Focus

In the beginning God created the heavens and the earth. ²The earth was formless and empty, and darkness covered the deep waters. And the Spirit of God was hovering over the surface of the waters.

³Then God said, "Let there be light," and there was light. ⁴And God saw that the light was good. The he separated the light from the darkness. ⁵God called the light "day" and darkness "night."

And evening passed and morning came, marking the first day. . . .

> ²⁷So God created human beings in his own image.
>   In the image of God he created them;
>   male and female he created them.

²⁸Then God blessed them and said, "Be fruitful and multiply. Fill the earth and govern it. Reign over the fish in the sea, the birds in the sky, and all the animals that scurry along the ground."

²⁹Then God said, "Look! I have given you every seed-bearing plant throughout the earth and all the fruit trees for your food. ³⁰And I have given every green plant as food for all the wild animals, the birds in the sky, and the small animals that scurry along the ground—everything that has life." And that is what happened.

³¹Then God looked over all he had made, and he saw that it was very good!

(Genesis 1:1-5, 27-31)

Reflect

Shortly after my first child, Alyssa, was born, I sat up late into the night holding her, studying every tiny detail. She was perfect. I had never seen anything so beautiful. No sunset, flower, mountain range, or seashore could compare to this amazing little creation. She was stunning. I was in awe.

It was a holy moment in that hospital room as I gazed into her little face. I thought of Genesis 1:31: "God looked over all he had made, and he saw that it was very good!" In that moment, she represented to me all of God's creation—perfect, beautiful, amazing to behold. So full of promise. My hopes for her life were grand. My dreams of what our relationship would be were precious.

But somewhere in the back of my mind, I knew that one day this little one would grow up. And part of growing up in this world would involve her making choices. Like you and me, she was born with the wonderful, dreadful, powerful gift of free will. This gift leads to both the opportunity to live closely with our Creator and the opportunity to distance ourselves from Him through sin.

I knew that, one day, my sweet girl and I would have times when we would enjoy close friendship, laughter, and joy, but there also would be moments that weren't as pleasant. Like all children, one day she would disobey me. She might color on the wall, talk back, or sneak out. As perfect as she appeared, she was also human, and that would surely bring us conflict at some point. But, knowing that didn't make me any less excited to have her in my life. She was my child, my precious girl. And I was so glad she was finally here.

I made Alyssa a promise that night. I promised her that no matter what happened in the future, I would not give up on her. I would love her, forgive her, and fight for her no matter what might come our way. It is a promise I will keep until the day I die.

This is a small glimpse of the kind of love our heavenly Father has for us! God's love not only endures the hard times but also pursues us in those times when we are distant.

God's love not only endures the hard times but also pursues us in those times when we are distant.

Who are you willing to love, forgive, and fight for no matter what?

How do you put that into practice?

Read Genesis 1. According to verse 31 (page 13), how did God describe all that He had made?

As I read the story of creation in Genesis 1, I wonder what God was thinking as He looked out upon all He had made. Scripture tells us that He looked across all of His creation and declared that it was very good. And I guess at that point, it was. But, since God is omniscient, He also had to know that this beautiful creation would also cause Him heartbreak. That we who were created in His image would disobey Him and treat Him with contempt at times. That some of His creation would reject Him entirely. Yet, He marveled anyway.

When have you marveled at creation? Perhaps it was a time when you were in the mountains or at the ocean. Describe the experience briefly below. Or draw a picture of something in creation that has filled you with awe.

The LORD your God is
with you,
  the Mighty Warrior
  who saves.
He will take great delight
in you;
  in his love he will no
  longer rebuke you,
  but will rejoice over
  you with singing.
    (Zephaniah 3:17 NIV)

———————————

God decided in advance to
adopt us into his own family
by bringing us to himself
through Jesus Christ. This is
what he wanted to do, and
it gave him great pleasure.
    (Ephesians 1:5)

———————————

For through him God
created everything
  in the heavenly realms
  and on earth.
He made the things we
can see
  and the things we
  can't see—
such as thrones, kingdoms,
rulers, and authorities in the
unseen world.
  Everything was created
  through him and for him.
    (Colossians 1:16)

There is plenty of time in our study to talk about the brokenness of creation, sin, and God's restoration plan. But for today, let's just marvel in the fact that after God made all that we are and all that we have, He sat back and said, "That's awesome!" Or to be specific, "Very good!"

> **Read Zephaniah 3:17 in the margin. According to this verse, how does God show His delight in us?**

What an amazing image! God is so delighted with you that He sings over you. The closest I can come to comprehending this is recalling the times I would stand over my babies' cribs and hum them to sleep. Those were precious, pure, and loving moments.

Have you ever stopped to ask the question, *Why did God create me*? Have you ever really pondered that?

The answer is beautifully simple. We were created so that God could enjoy a relationship with us! He was not content to live without us, so He created our world and put us here so that He could live in relationship with us. First John 3:1 (NIV) says, "See what great love the Father has lavished on us, that we should be called children of God! And that is what we are! The reason the world does not know us is that it did not know him." You were created to be loved by God. His plan since the beginning of time has been to adopt you into His family so that you and He can enjoy a pure and precious bond.

> **Read Ephesians 1:5 and Colossians 1:16 in the margin. What do these passages reveal to us about God's purpose for creation?**

These passages tell us that God created us with purpose. Notice in Colossians 1:16 it says that we were created through Him and for Him. The word *through* tells us that God's creative power generates our being. The word *for*, on the other hand, speaks to His relentless desire that we would draw close to Him in a loving relationship.

In Genesis 1 and 2, we see that God created a perfect environment. The world was new and untainted by sin. The relationship between God and His people was healthy and whole. This is why God was able to look upon everything and declare it very good.

How do you imagine God's perfect world before sin corrupted it? Jot down your thoughts and ideas below. Don't worry— there are no wrong answers!

Today we don't live in that perfect environment, but we can enjoy communion with God through Christ. This is the closest we will get to perfection in this lifetime. And as we'll see throughout this study, even when we begin to drift away from God, He pursues us and fights to bring us back to Himself. His passionate pursuit of us is what ties Scripture together from beginning to end. It is the underlying theme to every story, including yours. Let this penetrate deeply today: The God of the universe, the One who created sunsets and puppies, longs to be in fellowship with you.

Prayer

Dear God, thank You for the creativity and beauty of creation. As I begin this study, open my eyes to see the world as You see it. May my eyes see beauty as You do, and may my heart hurt over the brokenness in this world. I want to seek You with my whole heart so that we can be closer than ever before. Fill me with Your Spirit. In Jesus's name. Amen.

Day 2

Settle

Be still and thank God for the beauty of His creation. Specifically call out to Him those parts of our world that you find breathtaking. Marvel in Him and His creativity as you focus your attention on His presence today.

Focus

¹⁵The Lord God placed the man in the Garden of Eden to tend and watch over it. ¹⁶But the Lord God warned him, "You may freely eat the fruit of every tree in the garden— ¹⁷except the tree of the knowledge of good and evil. If you eat its fruit, you are sure to die."

(Genesis 2:15-17)

¹The serpent was the shrewdest of all the wild animals the Lord God had made. One day he asked the woman, "Did God really say you must not eat the fruit from any of the trees in the garden?"

²"Of course we may eat fruit from the trees in the garden," the woman replied. ³"It's only the fruit from the tree in the middle of the garden that we are not allowed to eat. God said, 'You must not eat it or even touch it; if you do, you will die.'"

⁴"You won't die!" the serpent replied to the woman. ⁵"God knows that your eyes will be opened as soon as you eat it, and you will be like God, knowing both good and evil."

⁶The woman was convinced. She saw that the tree was beautiful and its fruit looked delicious, and she wanted the wisdom it would give her. So she took some of the

fruit and ate it. Then she gave some to her husband, who was with her, and he ate it, too. ⁷At that moment their eyes were opened, and they suddenly felt shame at their nakedness.

(Genesis 3:1-7a)

Reflect

Lying is a big deal to me. No matter who or what the lie is about, or the motivation for the person telling it, a lie flips a switch in my mind. Once I discover that someone has lied to me, I always wonder if what that person is telling me is truthful moving forward. For instance, years ago I found that a friend had misled me by sharing only part of a story. The matter itself wasn't anything of great significance, but the fact that she intentionally deceived me was significant. It hurt me deeply. When I asked her about it, she sloughed it off as no big thing. I forgave her and asked her to be completely truthful in the future. By outward appearances, we went on as if nothing had happened. But something had happened.

Our relationship had been altered. I have forgiven her, but now I am cautious—and rightly so. Wisdom tells me to pay attention and to be sure I have all the facts when she shares information with me. This "little incident" changed our relationship. I still love her, but wisdom requires me to proceed in a different way until trust has been reestablished.

When and how has a relationship in your life been altered by sin?

How did you handle it?

How is your relationship different now?

"I don't want your sacrifices—I want your love; I don't want your offerings—I want you to know me."

(Hosea 6:6 TLB)

For the wages of sin is death, but the free gift of God is eternal life through Christ Jesus our Lord.

(Romans 6:23)

As we read the account in Genesis 3 of the first sin, it too may seem like a fairly insignificant event. I mean, this would be a misdemeanor, not a felony, right? It was just a piece of fruit. What's the big deal, God? The big deal is that God's command had been broken. Adam and Eve chose their will over God's, and that's called sin. Sin creates a wedge—a sense of separation— between us and God, and that, friend, is a very big deal.

Have you noticed that we humans have a tendency to downplay sin? Especially our own! Sin is uncomfortable to talk about, painful to confront, and difficult to overcome. The truth is, it's easier to move along quickly and trust that God will just give us a pass. Of course, God does give us a pass—called forgiveness—as we confess our sins to Him, but what He wants even more is for us to live in sync with His will.

Read Hosea 6:6 in the margin. In your own words, explain what this means:

Read Romans 6:23 in the margin and reflect on how the truth of this passage has affected your life in the past. When and how have you experienced "death" because of sin?

With the first bite of that forbidden fruit in the garden, this planet became infected with the virus of sin. And that infection has spread from one generation to the next with alarming strength. That simple act of rebellion put humanity on a new trajectory that creates separation between us and God. But at every turn, God has been offering pathways of redemption to us. He pursues us even in our rebellion, because His heart is to show us His love.

We don't know how long Eve lived, but Scripture tells us that Adam lived to be 930 years old (Genesis 5:5). That's a really long time. This means that Adam lived during the same time period of Noah's father. And it was during Noah's lifetime that humanity's sin reached a pinnacle.

Read Genesis 6:5-8 (NIV) below:

⁵The Lᴏʀᴅ saw how great the wickedness of the human race had become on the earth, and that every inclination of the thoughts of the human heart was only evil all the time. ⁶The Lᴏʀᴅ regretted that he had made human beings on the earth, and his heart was deeply troubled. ⁷So the Lᴏʀᴅ said, "I will wipe from the face of the earth the human race I have created— and with them the animals, the birds and the creatures that move along the ground—for I regret that I have made them." ⁸But Noah found favor in the eyes of the Lᴏʀᴅ.

How did the writer describe the human heart?

What did God regret, and what did He plan to do?

As Adam aged, he watched the world go from the perfection he had enjoyed in the garden to such depravity that the Scripture says God regretted ever having created humankind! The world was broken, and Adam and Eve were the ones who broke it! What responsibility. What heartache they must have felt.

Can you imagine when Noah's children were little and climbed onto Adam's and Eve's laps, saying, "Tell us about what it was like back in the beginning"? It was probably with deep sadness that they would recount the times of walking in the cool of the evening with God Himself. They had seen such change and decline in their lifetimes.

For all have sinned and fall short of the glory of God.
(Romans 3:23 NIV)

If we claim to be without sin, we deceive ourselves and the truth is not in us.
(1 John 1:8 NIV)

How have you seen moral decline in your lifetime?

How have these changes affected society?

On a more personal note, how has moral decay affected you and your family?

I have spent a lot of time thinking about what Adam and Eve must have felt in their later years. They watched one generation after the next fall deeper and deeper into the grip of sin. What guilt must they have carried. Surely, they wished their grandchildren could have been born into a world more like the one they first inhabited. How many times they must have wished for a do-over when it came to that dang fruit!

But as I think of Adam and Eve, I don't cast any stones because I know that if it had been me in that garden, I would have eventually been to blame too.

Read the Scriptures in the margin, and summarize what they tell us about sin:

When and how have you deceived yourself about your own sin? Describe one instance.

Paul says it pointedly in Romans 3:23: All have sinned. All! That's me and you. You, my friend, are a sinner. I am too. We have messed up. We carry the virus of sin. But as we will explore later this week, even in His children's disobedience, God did not give up on them. And that's good news. For today, let's marinate in the fact that we are sinners in need of pursuit.

While picking up food at a local restaurant, a young woman from church recognized me. I was embarrassed that I didn't know her by name, and I asked her to remind me who she was. She smiled shyly and said, "Oh, I haven't been to church in a long time." I encouraged her to come back, and I let her know that she is always welcome. Then she said something really interesting: "Well, I don't know. I've made a lot of mistakes. I don't know if there's any going back for me."

Her shame seemed to overwhelm her. I don't know her whole story, but I stopped what I was doing and looked her right in the eyes and said, "God loves you. No matter what has been going on, you can come back to Him." She only smiled, but she seemed to be listening and really taking it in.

A week later I was back at the same restaurant—same order, same girl. This time she greeted me with a hug and said, "Jen, I talked to my boyfriend, my sister, and my mom. We saw that you're having an outside service, and we're all coming! I'm not ready to go in the church doors yet, but one step at a time, right?"

I still don't know what transpired to make this beautiful young woman feel that her sin was so dark she could never come home to God. But it has been a privilege to watch joy restored in her life as she is reminded of how deeply she is loved and she rekindles her relationship with Christ.

Reread Genesis 3:1-7a (pages 18–19). What happens in verse 7, and what emotion do Adam and Eve feel in response?

When Adam's and Eve's eyes were opened, they suddenly felt shame. This was a new emotion for them—the shame and feeling of separation caused by sin. For today, let's make this personal.

God has the antidote for sin.

What sin is luring you away from God? Is it pride, apathy, greed, lust, anger, gossip, or something else?

Below, write a brief letter to God, confessing the sins He brings to mind, or simply list them as an act of worship and repentance:

Only three chapters into the Bible, we see the great virus of sin infect the whole human race. I am a carrier of this disease, and so are you. Yet, as we will see, God has the antidote for sin. He pursues us as a great and compassionate physician offering the vaccine to all who will turn to Him. And He does this out How have you seen moral decline in your lifetime?.

Prayer

Dear God, forgive me! For all of the times I have not lived into Your will, please forgive me. Thank You that Your mercies are new every day. I love You, and I am so thankful for Your unfailing love! Amen.

Day 3

Settle

As you direct your thoughts toward God, pray or even sing this Scripture back to Him:

> [10]*Create in me a clean heart, O God; and renew a right spirit within me.*
> [11]*Cast me not away from thy presence; and take not thy holy spirit from me.*
>
> [12]*Restore unto me the joy of thy salvation; and uphold me with thy free spirit.*
> (*Psalm 51:10-12 KJV*)

Focus

[11]*"Who told you that you were naked?" the* LORD *God asked. "Have you eaten from the tree whose fruit I commanded you not to eat?'"*

[12]*The man replied, "It was the woman you gave me who gave me the fruit, and I ate it."*

[13]*Then the* LORD *God asked the woman, "What have you done?"*

"The serpent deceived me," she replied. "That's why I ate it."

[14]*Then the* LORD *God said to the serpent,*

> *"Because you have done this, you are cursed*
>   *more than all animals, domestic and wild.*
> *You will crawl on your belly,*
>   *groveling in the dust as long as you live.*
> [15]*And I will cause hostility between you and the woman . . ."*

¹⁶*Then he said to the woman,*

"I will sharpen the pain of your pregnancy,
and in pain you will give birth.
And you will desire to control your husband,
but he will rule over you."

¹⁷*And to the man he said,*

"Since you listened to your wife and ate from the tree
whose fruit I commanded you not to eat,
the ground is cursed because of you.
All your life you will struggle to scratch a living from it."

(Genesis 3:11-17)

²³*Search me, God, and know my heart;*
test me and know my anxious thoughts.
²⁴*See if there is any offensive way in me,*
and lead me in the way everlasting.

(Psalm 139:23-24 NIV)

³*"Why do you look at the speck of sawdust in your brother's eye and pay no attention to the plank in your own eye?* ⁴*How can you say to your brother, 'Let me take the speck out of your eye,' when all the time there is a plank in your own eye?* ⁵*You hypocrite, first take the plank out of your own eye, and then you will see clearly to remove the speck from your brother's eye."*

(Matthew 7:3-5 NIV)

Reflect

Blaming others, even God, for our sins is not a new maneuver. One of my favorite stories of blame involves my daughter when she was just a toddler. As far as I know it was the first time she ever lied to me. And, as I revealed yesterday, lying is a big deal to me, so this was a serious offense. Here's what happened:

I went to put on some lace-up boots one morning—but the laces had been cut. That was odd. So, I went to my three-year-old Alyssa and asked if she knew how this had happened. She became very animated and said, "Oh, yes, it was a mouse." What? I stayed calm and said, "Well tell me about that."

She said, "Well, there was a mouse, and he did it; but it won't happen again cuz I squished him."

"So, where's the squished mouse?" I wanted to know.

She was quick with an answer, "His mommy mouse came and dragged him away." I wanted to believe my child. I didn't want to think she was lying. This had never happened between us before.

But she continued, "He cut the laces with mouse scissors, Mom." I was trying to believe her, could this have happened—but, mouse scissors, really?

Now I was aggravated, not about the boots, but about the lying. I sat Alyssa down gently and told her that she needed to tell me the truth. She stuck to her story. In fact, she doubled down with more details—there was even a mouse funeral. My sweet, cute, little girl blamed that little mouse with everything she had in her.

I was devastated. My little girl was a liar. She was not willing to take responsibility for her actions. Instead, she created a way to place the blame elsewhere. This little episode rocked my world. I called my husband, Jim, crying. "She's a little liar. There was a mouse and my boots and mouse scissors..." It took him a moment to catch on and then he said very wisely, "Well, she gets this from us, honey. We're sinners."

Alyssa faced consequences for cutting the laces, for placing blame somewhere else, and most of all, for the lying. Sin has consequences. We wanted her to discover early in life that when we sin, we have to own it, repent of it, and try to set things right.

But that is hard, isn't it? Perhaps, it is pride that keeps us from taking responsibility for our own sins and shortcomings. Perhaps, we would just rather live in denial. Or perhaps, it's just so much easier to recognize sin in someone else's life than it is to see it in our own.

When have you blamed others, or even your circumstances, for the sin in your life?

How have you blamed God in the past for your own poor behavior?

Look back at Genesis 3:12-13 (page 25). How do we see blame pass from one to the other? Complete the following:

1. _____ blames _____ for

_____ .

2. _____ blames _____ for

_____ .

3. Look again at verse 12. How does Adam even cast blame on God?

Sin is like a cancer. It can grow and become part of the very fabric of our beings. In fact, it doesn't take long at all to become very comfortable with our particular varieties of sin.

As Jesus is preaching, He warns us to be careful of falling into a trap regarding our sin.

Reread Matthew 7:3-5 (page 26). What trap does Jesus describe in these verses?

God stands ready to offer us forgiveness. Jesus's grace has already been extended to us, but it is not a cheap grace. It has come at a price—that of God's own Son. Therefore, we must be diligent not to fall into the dangerous trap of complacency about sin; we must examine our own lives regularly and call out to God to be set right according to His standards. David does this when he cries out to God, saying,

Answers: 1. Adam / Eve / giving him the fruit 2. Eve / serpent / deceiving her 3. Adam says God gave him the woman.

²³ *Search me, God, and know my heart;*
   test me and know my anxious thoughts.
²⁴ *See if there is any offensive way in me,*
   and lead me in the way everlasting.
               (Psalm 139:23-24 NIV)

This is a vulnerable prayer from David, but surely it honors God. He is crying out, saying essentially, "Reveal to me what is wrong in my life and help me live in a way that brings a smile to Your face." No wonder David is described in Acts 13:22 as a man after God's own heart. There is no blaming, no excuses. David is vulnerable, opening himself up fully before the Lord and inviting God to reveal to him anything in need of correction.

When I think back to the day of the mouse scissor fiasco, two things stand out to me: Alyssa's stubborn but creative response to her actions, and Jim's words on the phone: "She gets this from us. We're sinners." I too can become stubborn, and even creative, when it comes to justifying my less than honorable thoughts and actions. I can fall into the blame game wanting it to be someone, anyone, else's fault. Thank goodness we serve a God who loves us in spite of our excuses. His grace is available no matter what we've done, and His arms are open to welcome us at every moment.

We serve a God who loves us in spite of our excuses.

Prayer

- Pray Psalm 139:23-24 to God, personalizing it for your life and circumstances:

   Search me, O God, and know my heart [about _____];
      test me and know my anxious thoughts [about _____]
   Point out anything in me that offends you [such as _____],
      and lead me along the path of everlasting life.

- Pause as you pray, listening for whatever the Holy Spirit might bring up for you, or pray the Scripture through and then sit in stillness and silence for a few minutes. Allow God to speak to you about the things (sins) He'd like you to notice. What invitations do you hear?

Day 4

Settle

What brings you joy? Singing, drawing, being outside, writing, playing an instrument? Do that today and allow God to speak to you in that activity.

Focus

[22]*Then the Lord God said, "Look, the human being have become like us, knowing both good and evil. What if they reach out, take fruit from the tree of life, and eat it? Then they will live forever!"* [23]*So the Lord God banished them from the Garden of Eden, and he sent Adam out to cultivate the ground from which he had been made.* [24]*After sending them out, the Lord God stationed mighty cherubim to the east of the Garden of Eden. And he placed a flaming sword that flashed back and forth to guard the way to the tree of life.*

(Genesis 3:22-24 NLT)

[8]*"For my thoughts are not your thoughts,*
   neither are your ways my ways,"
      declares the Lord.
[9]*"As the heavens are higher than the earth,*
   so are my ways higher than your ways
   and my thoughts than your thoughts."
      (Isaiah 55:8-9 NIV)

Reflect

In high school I didn't have very strong self-esteem. Like most teenage girls, I didn't think I was pretty enough, smart enough, popular enough—

anything enough. So, when my first boyfriend broke up with me in tenth grade, I felt like my fears must be reality. I just wasn't enough.

It was a sad time. But something very interesting began to happen in my life during that sad season. You see, I began to receive anonymous flowers. It began with a homecoming corsage delivered to me at school signed simply, "With love, Your best boyfriend." I had no idea where it had come from. It became the talk of my classroom.

A few months later, on Valentine's Day, I received flowers again at school—same signature, "Your best boyfriend." Now more than my classmates were talking. It was a real mystery. Was this a friend, a secret admirer, the former jerk boyfriend? I truly had no idea. But the flowers continued through high school. I became convinced that my best friend, who was a guy, was behind it. But he always promised that he wasn't. My best boyfriend remained a mystery.

When I went off to college, I was absolutely shocked when a bouquet of roses showed up at my dorm with the same signature—"Your best boyfriend." I was dating someone, no not my husband, but still I had a boyfriend and I knew he hadn't sent them. The flowers continued until my junior year of college.

I remember exactly because I received my last bouquet from my secret admirer the day after my husband, Jim, asked me to marry him. This time the card was signed slightly differently—"With love, Your second best boyfriend, Dad."

Wow! It had never occurred to me that my dad would have gone to the trouble to send those flowers. When I was in high school, we didn't talk much. He grew up with three brothers, and I was a depressed teenage girl. He didn't know what to do with me, and I didn't know how to relate to him. So, we mostly coexisted during those years. But, even in that time when we had a hard time connecting, he found a way to make me feel loved. And, when the time was right, he let me know that he had been there all along.

In his quiet way, Dad was pursuing me, and for that I am forever grateful. Our heavenly Father does the same thing. Even when we feel distant, even when we don't understand His ways, He is there for us. Even before we come to believe in Him, God's grace is at work in our lives. This is called prevenient grace, which is a fancy term for God at work in our lives even before we acknowledge Him.

> **As you look back on your life, in what ways can you see God guiding you, looking out for you, even when you were not looking for Him?**

After their disobedience, Adam and Eve were driven from the garden of Eden. They had enjoyed precious times with their Creator. These were times of pure peace and joy, but that had been interrupted by a willful act of disobedience. They, like us, became convinced that they knew better than God what was best for them, and they made a choice against God's law. Those choices, known as sin, have consequences.

> **Read again the Scripture from our devotional lesson yesterday, Genesis 3:11-17 (pages 25–26). What were the consequences Adam and Eve received individually?**
>
> **Eve:**
>
>
> **Adam:**
>
>
> **Now read Genesis 3:22-24 (page 30). What was the shared consequence for Adam and Eve?**

They had to leave their idyllic setting. Now, imagine you are Eve. What are you thinking and feeling as the angels escort you out of the only home you've ever known? Your new surroundings will require work, and the perfect relationship with God you enjoyed in the garden has been broken. It's not severed, but it's just not the same since that bite of fruit!

Surely, Eve was sorry; repentant, even. But sin causes us to feel separated from God. It does not, however, have to end the relationship with our Creator. The precious part of this story to me is that what seems like discipline is actually God extending love and mercy to His children.

If Adam and Eve had continued in the garden and eaten from the tree of life, they would have lived forever and been forever estranged from God. Usually living forever would sound like a great thing, right? But, Scripture indicates that living in a fallen world forever is too great a penalty. God would rather them come to be with Him back in a paradise setting: heaven. So, in His mercy, God set a guard beside the tree and moved Adam and Eve to a new neighborhood.

Changing subdivisions, leaving the garden of Eden, was not on their radar. They had a great thing going. But once sin entered the picture, God knew that living forever in a world where sin had been unleashed would be too heavy a burden for His precious children to bear. Leaving the garden was actually a protection, from a loving Father, in a difficult situation.

> Read Isaiah 55:8-9 (page 30). When have you struggled to give up your plan and embrace God's plan for your life?

> Looking back, can you see any evidence of God's love and mercy in that particular time or circumstance? If so, describe it below. If not, how have you grown or changed as a result of the experience?

Even when we are hurting and distant, God stands ready to receive us when we turn to Him.

As I look back at my relationship with Dad in those teenage years, I realize that we were living in a semi-broken state, and he was not content with that. So, he loved me and pursued me, even when I gave him no credit for it. Even when I showed no interest in deepening a relationship with him, Dad was reaching out. How precious is that? Thank you, Daddy.

God does the same for us. Though we don't deserve it, He continually pursues us. Even when we are hurting and distant, God stands ready to receive us when we turn to Him. It's often only in retrospect that we see how He has looked out for us and sought us out throughout our lives. We can be thankful for a God who loves us that much!

Prayer

- Thank God for His ongoing presence in your life. Praise Him that even when you don't understand His ways, you acknowledge that His ways are better than your own.

- Turn Jeremiah 29:13 into a prayer like this: "I will seek You and find You when I seek You with all my heart."

Day 5

Settle

Set a timer for two minutes and just be still. In the silence, ask God to allow His peace and presence to settle upon you.

Focus

¹*In the beginning God created the heavens and the earth. ²The earth was formless and empty, and darkness covered the deep waters. And the Spirit of God was hovering over the surface of the waters.*

³*Then God said, "Let there be light," and there was light. ⁴And God saw that the light was good. The He separated the light from the darkness. ⁵God called the light "day" and darkness "night."*

And evening passed and morning came, marking the first day.

(Genesis 1:3-5)

¹⁶*For God so loved the world that he gave his one and only Son, that whoever believes in him shall not perish but have eternal life. ¹⁷For God did not send his Son into the world to condemn the world, but to save the world through him.*

(John 3:16-17 NIV)

For now we see through a glass, darkly; but then face to face: now I know in part; but then shall I know even as also I am known.

(1 Corinthians 13:12 KJV)

²¹*So you see, just as death came into the world through a man, now the resurrection from the dead has begun through another man. ²²Just as everyone dies because we all belong to Adam, everyone who belongs to Christ will be given new life.*

(1 Corinthians 15:21-22)

Reflect

When I first sit down to begin writing a book, devotion, or sermon, I often stare at the blank page or screen completely paralyzed. I am overwhelmed at the nothingness that currently exists. There is an idea or a goal, but on the page, there is nothing. There is excitement at the possibility of what might be created, but there also is an overwhelming sense of void. In that moment, I pause and ask God to speak. I need Him to generate ideas, to bring Scripture and stories to mind, to fuel the creative spark and help me organize thoughts into something that might bless someone else.

This is God's specialty. He is the master of creation. God speaks, and from nothing comes everything. Just from God speaking! That is amazing. The earth and skies, the orchids and the lilies, the giraffe and the hippopotamus come into being through God's creative spark.

Can you imagine the joy God must have experienced as He watched the animals graze and the butterflies flit, the dolphins jump and the elephants trumpet? What fulfillment He must have felt watching as Adam rejoiced when he first met Eve. I love Genesis 2:23 where Adam exclaims "At last!" which very loosely translates, "She's awesome!" God intended for His creations to enjoy perfect harmony with one another and their Creator.

God wanted us all to enjoy the perfection of Eden. But with the introduction of sin, that harmony was changed. Now, we are only able to enjoy glimpses of that perfection: "For now we see through a glass, darkly; but then face to face: now I know in part; but then shall I know even as also I am known" (1 Corinthians 13:12 KJV).

In my parents' home is an antique mirror that has clouded with age. When you peer into it, you get just a vague reflection of what is actually there. It is a distorted, blurry, partial image. When I gaze into that mirror, I think of this verse. We are only able to have glimpses of what it will be like to live in perfect harmony with God and one another. Today, we only catch partial views of what our Creator originally intended. It is like looking through a glass darkly—the real image isn't quite visible.

Friend, you were made for more than peering through a darkened glass. God wants more for you than vague glimpses of heaven. He pursues you so that you can one day call heaven home and know the perfect Eden-like environment that He first established for His creation.

I often wonder what it will be like in heaven. What will our relationship with Jesus be like? What will it be like to talk with the people we have known only vaguely through Scripture such as Deborah, Sarah, and the woman at the well? What will it feel like to live in a perfect environment where there is no pollution, erosion, or deforestation? What will it be like to enjoy relationships void of anger, jealousy, and pettiness? That seems so foreign to what we experience today.

Read Revelation 21:4-8 and 22:1-5. What images do these passages give you about heaven? Write or draw your response below.

God's creation is now born into a broken world that only vaguely resembles what God originally intended. But God's children, those who are adopted into His family, will experience that perfection one day in heaven. There is a distinction between God's creation and God's children. Everyone is a part of God's creation, but to be a child of God means being adopted into His family. That happens the moment we repent of our sins and receive Jesus, God's Son, as our Lord and Savior. At that moment, we are justified by our faith.

But to all who believed him and accepted him, he gave the right to become children of God.

(John 1:12)

See how very much our Father loves us, for he calls us his children, and that is what we are! But the people who belong to this world don't recognize that we are God's children because they don't know him.

(1 John 3:1)

---

16 For God so loved the world that he gave his one and only Son, that whoever believes in him shall not perish but have eternal life. 17 For God did not send his Son into the world to condemn the world, but to save the world through him.

(John 3:16-17 NIV)

When teaching my children about justification, I told them it simply means that it is just as if they had never sinned. Justification brings about a cleansing of all of our sins—past, present, and future—and enters us into the process of growing into the likeness of God's Son, our older brother in the faith family, Jesus.

Read John 1:12 and 1 John 3:1 in the margin. What do these verses mean to you?

You and I are born as God's creations, and God loves His created beings. But we have the opportunity to be more—to become part of God's family, God's adopted children. And that brings with it the promise of an eternity with God, both now on earth and in heaven. This is God's ultimate pursuit. He was not content to live without us eternally, so Jesus came to earth. John 3:16-17 are perhaps the most famous verses in Scripture. They clearly communicate to us how passionately our heavenly Father pursues us.

In fact, I like to think of these verses as a covert mission on which a loving Father sends His specially equipped Son in order to rescue the rest of the family, going to whatever lengths are required in order to bring them home.

It may be that you've heard John 3:16-17 so often that the verses no longer wow you. Sometimes that happens when things become familiar. But these verses powerfully summarize God's relentless pursuit of us.

Read John 3:16-17 in the margin, and rewrite the verses below in your own words:

One amazing thing about this passage is the promise contained within it: eternal life. But there is also a premise, or condition, which must be met in order for the promise to be claimed: believing in Jesus as the Son of God.

This week we have seen how sin disrupted the perfection that God created for us. But, we have also seen that, as a loving Father, God continually creates a pathway back to Him— ultimately, not even sparing His own Son at the cross in order for us to live in unbroken fellowship with Him. Paul describes this process and relationship beautifully in his Letter to the Corinthians.

As a loving Father, God continually creates a pathway back to Him.

Read 1 Corinthians 15:21-22 in the margin. What does this verse promise those who belong to Christ?

[21]So you see, just as death came into the world through a man, now the resurrection from the dead has begun through another man. [22]Just as everyone dies because we all belong to Adam, everyone who belongs to Christ will be given new life.

(1 Corinthians 15:21-22)

Who in your life needs to be given new life? How can you reach out to them?

From the very beginning, God has pursued His people. He created a perfect environment for us, but it was tainted by sin. The great news is that there is another perfect home awaiting all who call upon Jesus as Lord of their lives: heaven. This week we have looked at Creation, the Fall, and Redemption. At every step, one thing remains the same: The Creator of the universe pursues His creation with a relentless love. His goal, His joy, is that all would come to know and love Him as He knows and loves us. As we close our study this week, I hope that you will take the time to thank Him for this loving pursuit—and make it personal!

Prayer

- Read 1 John 3:1 and take the time to thank God for pursuing you and adopting you into His family.

- If you have never asked God to forgive you of your sins and become Lord of your life, you may want to pray something like the prayer below and move from creation to child of God today!

  Dear God, thank You for loving me and pursuing me. Please forgive me of my sins. I receive Jesus, Your Son, as Lord of my life. Wash me clean and help me to live in ways that please You. I love You. Help me to know and love You more. Amen.

If you do pray to receive Jesus as your Savior today, please contact me at jennifercowart.org. I'd love to pray for you and celebrate with you!

Video Viewer Guide
WEEK 1

Scriptures: Genesis 1:1-2, Genesis 1:24-28a, 31, Genesis 3:1-6a, Genesis 3:11-13, Genesis 3:22-24

God does not _____ _____ on us.

God _____ us in our lives each day.

The God of the universe _____ _____ you.

Pursued through Growing Pains

PATRIARCHS AND MATRIARCHS OF THE FAITH

Day 1

Settle

Stand up and stretch for a minute or two. Take a few deep breaths and relax for a moment. As you settle in, pause and allow your mind to slow down and just be still before the Lord today.

Focus

³¹What, then, shall we say in response to these things? If God is for us, who can be against us? ³²He who did not spare his own Son, but gave him up for us all—how will he not also, along with him, graciously give us all things? ³³Who will bring any charge against those whom God has chosen? It is God who justifies. ³⁴Who then is the one who condemns? No one. Christ Jesus who died—more than that, who was raised to life—is at the right hand of God and is also interceding for us. ³⁵Who shall separate us from the love of Christ? Shall trouble or hardship or persecution or famine or nakedness or danger or sword? ³⁶As it is written:

"For your sake we face death all day long;
   we are considered as sheep to be slaughtered."

³⁷No, in all these things we are more than conquerors through him who loved us.

(Romans 8:31-37 NIV)

¹The LORD had said to Abram, "Leave your native country, your relatives, and your father's family, and go to the land that I will show you. ²I will make you into a great nation. I will bless you and make you famous, and you will be a blessing to others. ³I will bless those who bless you and curse those who treat you with contempt. All the families on earth will be blessed through you."

⁴So Abram departed as the LORD had instructed.

(Genesis 12:1-4)

¹*Faith is the confidence that what we hope for will actually happen; it gives us assurance about things we cannot see.* ²*Through their faith, the people in days of old earned a good reputation.*

³*By faith we understand that the entire universe was formed at God's command, that what we now see did not come from anything that can be seen.*

(Hebrews 11:1-3)

⁸*It was by faith that Abraham obeyed when God called him to leave home and go to another land that God would give him as his inheritance. He went without knowing where he was going.* ⁹*And even when he reached the land God promised him, he lived there by faith—for he was like a foreigner, living in tents. And so did Isaac and Jacob, who inherited the same promise.*

(Hebrews 11:8-9)

Reflect

In the sixth grade I somehow mustered up the courage to try out for the cheerleading squad. I'll spare you the details, but as a shy middle schooler, I never stood a chance. In short, I was not chosen. It wasn't devastating, it was worse. It was confirming. As I shared last week I struggled in middle and high school to feel like I was enough—popular enough, good enough, athletic enough, pretty enough, outgoing enough. Not being chosen to cheerlead was confirmation that I once again was not enough. It was another nail in the coffin of my adolescent self-esteem.

When have you felt rejection in the past? How did it affect you?

When have your fears of rejection held you back?

How have those fears affected your spiritual life?

My fears of failure and what others might think often held me back, but when I went off to college I decided it was time for a change. I made a conscious decision to be more outgoing. I was going to try new things, initiate friendships, and seek out new adventures. It was more than an emotional decision to be courageous though; it was a spiritual act of faith. As a young follower of Christ, I knew that God chose me; it was other people who I wasn't so sure about. My fears had held me back so many times in the past. College was an opportunity to live with a new freedom as a chosen daughter of God. I had to trust my faith more than my fears in those first days of stepping out into new opportunities. It was a pivotal point in my life.

Read Romans 8:31-37 (page 43). What feelings of comfort do you experience from this passage?

This week we will look at superstars of the Old Testament. These matriarchs and patriarchs of the faith were not perfect, but they, like you, were chosen. Today our focus is on a power couple of Genesis—Abraham and Sarah. If you grew up in church you know their stories. In fact, you may have sung the song, "Father Abraham, had many sons, many sons had father Abraham..." This song points to the many faiths that emerge from Abraham's descendants. The Jewish, Christian, and Muslim people all trace their origins back to Father Abraham.

Let's review their story. In Genesis 12, God chooses Abram and his wife, Sarai, above everyone on earth. I've often wondered what it was about them that made God choose them. As we read about Abram and Sarai, their names are later changed to Abraham and Sarah (Genesis 17), but nothing else really stands out. It's not like they were the wisest or most talented people of their time. We don't see a long, distinguished line of heroes from which they emerge. What sets them apart?

Read Genesis 12:1-4 (page 43). What did God tell Abram and Sarai to do?

What was their response?

Apparently, the thing that is unique about Abram and Sarai is that they are faithful and available. When God pursues them and invites them into partnership with His plans, they say yes. When God says, "Let's go!" they say, "Yes, Sir!" They didn't even know where they were headed! God just says, "Go to the land that I will show you," and they pack up and start walking! Surely, they had questions. Didn't Sarai have some fears about what lay ahead? Did they feel they were up to the task?

Perhaps, they had many fears and lots of questions. Maybe they were concerned that they would not be enough, like me in middle school. But when God chose them, they responded. They were fully available and faithfully obedient. That's a great recipe for a life that God can use.

When have you made yourself fully available to God? What was the outcome?

As a church leader I have had the opportunity to work with lots of talented, precious people over the years. But I have learned that the most talented and most outgoing people are not always the wisest hires. In fact, I'll take faithful and obedient to God's standards over mega-talented any day. Don't get me wrong, both in one package is pretty terrific, but if there is a choice to be made? Humble and hard-working with a hunger to please God wins! Abraham seems to fall into this classification.

God does extraordinary things through ordinary people who put their trust in Him. Think about all of the ordinary men and women who become biblical superstars: David, a shepherd boy; Moses, a child born during a genocide; Esther, a poor Jewish girl living in a foreign land; Joseph, a carpenter in tiny Nazareth; and Peter, an uneducated fisherman from the Galilee region. These folks have one thing in common: when God pursued them, they responded to Him in faith.

God does extraordinary things through ordinary people who put their trust in Him.

Read Hebrews 11. This chapter is devoted to honoring those who were faithful in following God's calling in their lives. Next to the names in the chart on the following page, write down what these people did in faith.

PERSON	WHAT THEY DID IN FAITH
Abel (v. 4)	
Noah (v. 7)	
Moses's parents (v. 23)	
Moses (vv. 24-25)	
Israelites (v. 29)	
Israelite army (v. 30)	
Rahab (v. 31)	

If this chapter were to be expanded to include *your* story, how would you hope it reads? Write your name and story of responding in faith below:

It was by faith that _____ ...
(your name)

It's comforting to me that Abraham and Sarah were chosen for what appear to be simple reasons: availability and faithfulness. Our culture often chooses those who are good looking, charismatic, intelligent, wealthy, or talented. But God looks for different qualifications, and that is good news for us. Perhaps, being available and faithful sound ordinary and simple. But God often uses ordinary people in extraordinary ways when they respond to His pursuit of them.

When is a time you have felt God calling and pursuing you?

How did you respond?

When God called Abraham and Sarah, along with the other greats of Scripture like Deborah, Noah, and Esther, they each had a decision to make. Would they make themselves available for His plans and His purposes? Would they respond to His pursuit of them? Would they be faithful even when they didn't feel qualified?

We have that same choice to make today. Rest assured, God is pursuing you! He passionately loves you and invites you to partner with Him in amazing adventures during your lifetime. Surely, you will feel unqualified at times. You will, most likely, find excuses and suggest to God that He choose someone else. But don't do that! Instead, lean into His calling and watch what God will do with someone who is faithful and available.

Prayer

- Spend a few moments in silence simply focusing your heart and mind on God's presence.
- It may seem silly, but try this anyway: Wrap your arms around yourself and say aloud, "I am chosen by God." I know, it seems silly, but really do it anyway. It's a hug from God today! Plus, who couldn't use an extra hug?
- As you pray today thank God for His faithful love toward you and offer yours in return to Him.

Day 2

Settle

Begin your time with God by listening to "The Father's House" by Cory Asbury or another worship song of your choosing.

Focus

¹Some time later, the LORD spoke to Abram in a vision and said to him, "Do not be afraid, Abram, for I will protect you, and your reward will be great."

²But Abram replied, "O Sovereign LORD, what good are all your blessings when I don't even have a son? Since you have given me no children, Eliezer of Damascus, a servant in my household, will inherit all my wealth. ³You have given me no descendants of my own, so one of my servants will be my heir."

⁴Then the LORD said to him, "No, your servant will not be your heir, for you will have a son of your own who will be your heir." ⁵Then the LORD took Abram outside and said to him, "Look up into the sky and count the stars if you can. That's how many descendants you will have!"

⁶And Abram believed the LORD, and the LORD counted him as righteous because of his faith.

(Genesis 15:1-6)

¹Sarai, Abram's wife, had not been able to bear children for him. But she had an Egyptian servant named Hagar. ²So Sarai said to Abram, "The LORD has prevented me from having children. Go and sleep with my servant. Perhaps I can have children through her." And Abram agreed with Sarai's proposal.

(Genesis 16:1-2)

⁷"I will confirm my covenant with you and your descendants after you, from generation to generation. This is the everlasting covenant: I will always be your God and the God of your descendants after you. ⁸And I will give you the entire land of Canaan, where you now live as a foreigner, to you and your descendants. It will be their possession forever, and I will be their God."

(Genesis 17:7-8)

The LORD is close to the brokenhearted;
    he rescues those whose spirits are crushed.
                  (Psalm 34:18)

(If you have time, go ahead and read all of Genesis 15–17 for the context of today's story.)

Reflect

I have a parenting trick that I want to share with you. It worked like magic with my kids when their attitudes or behavior fell below the Cowart standard. (They're young adults now, and this tactic still has moments of wonder!) Here's how it works: when things are going badly, be pleasant, stay unemotional, and just say no. I learned this from Kevin Leman's book *Have a New Kid by Friday*, and friends, this is gold!

Let me illustrate. Let's say your precious child has had a bad attitude, then comes to you wanting to go to a friend's house to play. In a pleasant voice, you simply say no. Or if your fifth grader has been slow to get homework done, or even worse, just hasn't been doing it, but now he wants to go to a movie. When he asks to go, you smile and say no. Now, this isn't always easy, and we all mess up at times. But with practice and lots of grace (for ourselves and for our kids), we can learn to be less emotional.

For years I would get so upset, even personally offended, when my children weren't making good decisions. Then I discovered that I could love them passionately without hopping onto an emotional roller coaster. It was possible to deliver appropriate discipline by simply putting logical consequences in place for their actions. And, you know what? It worked.

I remember a time when my teenage daughter was particularly moody and had not treated her dad and me with much respect. She was hoping to have friends over for the weekend, but we told her no with a smile. She then asked if she could go to the movies. Again, no. Saturday morning she wanted to go on a walk. No. By Saturday afternoon she had heard so many no's that all she wanted was to sit on the couch with us and snuggle. This we said yes to! She was no longer interested in what we could do for her, she simply wanted to restore the relationship. This was our goal.

It would have been easier to say yes, honestly. So often, in tough situations, the easy way out is to give in. But real love does hard things.

With my son, there was a great moment when after not turning in an assignment, he actually asked to go to a party. I said, "Oh buddy, I wish you could go! That sounds so fun. But, since you didn't get your paper in, no, you can't go. Maybe next time you'll have all your stuff done so you can be there. I'll try to help you remember, if you want me to." He just looked at me for a moment, and then said, "Yeah, maybe next time you can help me stay on track." He actually invited me into the process with him when practical discipline was put into place.

Here's the point: There are logical consequences to rebellious behavior, but it doesn't mean that in our rebellion we are not loved.

Those whom I love I rebuke and discipline. So be earnest and repent.

(Revelation 3:19 NIV)

Read Revelation 3:19 in the margin. What does it say about the connection between love and discipline?

Scripture teaches us again and again that discipline is a sign of love. Note, however, that discipline and punishment are very different. Discipline is meant to correct a behavior. Punishment is meant to penalize. Perhaps, there are times for both, but discipline offered in love is the most effective means of maintaining a healthy relationship while offering correction.

Read Genesis 15:1-6 and Genesis 16:1-2 (page 50). What was God's promise to Abram and Sarai?

How did Abram and Sarai respond when it seemed like God had not kept His promise?

Abram and Sarai took matters into their own hands when they decided to have a child through Hagar. Although they seemed to believe that God's ultimate goal of a nation would come to pass, they did not wait on God's timing to see it happen through Sarai. Their lack of patient obedience resulted in consequences that were far reaching. Hagar and her son, Ishmael, eventually separate from the family. But God still blessed them. Ishmael became the father of a great nation of people, the Ishmaelites.

Although Sarai and Abram were disobedient, God's love for them did not waiver. In life, we will experience hard times for various reasons. Sometimes our poor decisions result in negative consequences. Sometimes God allows us to go through a tough time in order to refine our character. And sometimes, because we live on a broken planet, bad things happen through no fault of our own and we go through hard times. Whatever the case may be, there is a constant: God is with you, pursuing you, wanting to comfort you in your distress. In fact, Psalm 34:18 (NIV) promises us that "the Lord is close to the brokenhearted and saves those who are crushed in spirit."

Read another one of Abraham and Sarah's adventure in Genesis 20.

What deception did Abraham plot for Abimelek?

Why do you think Abraham and Sarah lied in this way?

How was Abraham's scheme uncovered?

How do you think Abraham felt when Abimelek confronted him?

How did God bless Abraham and Sarah despite their lack of faith?

When have you disappointed God?

How did you feel His presence even in that difficult time?

As we saw yesterday, God chose Abraham and Sarah because they were available and faithful. But as we read today, they were far from perfect. For instance, they were not patient for God's timing to have children. And in fear, Abraham misled Abimelek about his relationship with Sarah. Why would God use people who had these types of flaws?

The answer is simple: All God has to choose from is flawed people! Even when we make ourselves available and when we do our best to be faithful like Abraham and Sarah, we will not reach perfection this side of heaven. There will be times when we mess up. And like a good parent, there will be times when God disciplines us in order to refine our character. But even in our moments of redirection, we can know that God loves us relentlessly. It's the loving parent who takes the time and effort to discipline and redirect his or her child. Even in our imperfections, the God of the universe, our heavenly Father pursues us! That's great news!

In both situations where we see Abraham sin, in his impatience with children and his fear about his wife, God redeems him. God is there with him. There are consequences, but God does not abandon or turn His back on those He loves—and that's all of us! Instead, He pursues us. He loves us in the hard moments, just like I did when my kids got in trouble.

God pursues us with an unwavering, unconditional love. There is great comfort in knowing that nothing we think or do can separate us from Him. In our imperfect states, we are loved. We are pursued! Thank you, God!

Prayer

Cry out to God today with a thankful heart. You may want to even list all of the ways He has blessed you in your lifetime. Make today's prayer one of pure thanksgiving, not asking Him for anything. Just thank Him for who He is and what He has done!

> **Even in our moments of redirection, we can know that God loves us relentlessly.**

Day 3

Settle

What do you enjoy doing? Try starting your time with the Lord in a new way today. Take a walk, stretch, sing to Him, play an instrument, or draw. As you do whatever you may choose, dedicate the time to Him and just enjoy His presence. Whatever you do, do it unto the Lord (Colossians 3:23).

Focus

> [19]*This is the account of the family of Isaac, the son of Abraham.* [20]*When Isaac was forty years old, he married Rebekah.... * [21]*Isaac pleaded with the LORD on behalf of his wife, because she was unable to have children. The LORD answered Isaac's prayer, and Rebekah became pregnant with twins.*
>
> (Genesis 25:19-21)

> [27]*As the boys grew up, Esau became a skillful hunter. He was an outdoorsman, but Jacob had a quiet temperament, preferring to stay at home.* [28]*Isaac loved Esau because he enjoyed eating the wild game Esau brought home, but Rebekah loved Jacob.*

> [29]*One day when Jacob was cooking some stew, Esau arrived home from the wilderness exhausted and hungry.* [30]*Esau said to Jacob, "I'm starved! Give me some of that red stew!" (This is how Esau got his other name, Edom, which means "red.")*

> [31]*"All right," Jacob replied, "but trade me your rights as the firstborn son."*

> [32]*"Look, I am dying of starvation!" said Esau. "What good is my birthright to me now?"*

³³But Jacob said, "First you must swear that your birthright is mine." So Esau swore an oath, thereby selling all his rights as the firstborn to his brother, Jacob.

³⁴Then Jacob gave Esau some bread and lentil stew.

(Genesis 25:27-34a)

(Read Genesis 27 to see how Jacob received the blessing of his father, Isaac.)

See to it that no one fails to obtain the grace of God; that no "root of bitterness" spring up and causes trouble.

(Hebrews 12:15 ESV)

Get rid of all bitterness, rage and anger, brawling and slander, along with every form of malice.

(Ephesians 4:31 NIV)

Reflect

I grew up the oldest of three children. My two younger brothers are awesome, but I always felt a little badly about the fact that I was obviously my parent's favorite. It seemed to me that I got the most attention and the most praise. My parents were always there for me. Surely, my brothers noticed! I hoped they didn't resent it.

So it was interesting that as young adults when we were recounting childhood stories, we each mentioned that we knew that we were the favorite. Both of my brothers felt the way I did! They thought they were each my parents' favorite child because of the love they felt was lavished upon them. (Now in all honesty, I do think my baby brother got away with more than we did, but still I thought I was the favorite.)

I was amazed at my parents' skills in parenting. As a young parent myself, I thought it was pretty incredible that my parents had loved each of us so well that we each felt we were the favored child. When we asked them about it, they laughed and said we were all right—each one of us was the favorite. Mom and Dad were intentional to love us well in ways that we each could understand. They pursued us. They became interested in what we were interested in. For me, music; my older brother, cars; my younger brother, building things. My mom and dad adapted their parenting to match our personalities and the result was that we felt cherished.

Who has made you feel special in life?

How can you make those close to you feel precious and chosen today?

If only some of the parents in the Old Testament could have learned a lesson or two from my mom and dad's playbook.

Abraham and Sarah obviously showed Isaac favor. Ishmael, Abraham's oldest son, is sent away with his mother, Hagar, while Isaac is given Abraham's full inheritance and blessing (Genesis 21:8-21). That one action created great divisions that have lasting effects today. Isaac, the favored son of his parents, then shows favoritism to his eldest twin son, Esau. Rebekah, Isaac's wife, on the other hand, favors their younger child, Jacob. As Scripture tells us in Genesis 25:28: "Isaac loved Esau because he enjoyed eating the wild game Esau brought home, but Rebekah loved Jacob."

Have you ever felt the pain of not feeling favored or chosen with your family? Explain.

If so, how has it affected you?

Favoritism, especially in families, causes pain. When that favoritism leads to deception, like it did with Jacob and Esau, the results are even more damaging. Genesis 27:41 leaves no doubt about how favoritism affected these brothers: "From that time on, Esau hated Jacob because their father had given Jacob the blessing. And Esau began to scheme: 'I will soon be mourning my father's death. *Then* I will kill my brother, Jacob.'"

Isaac and Rebekah playing favorites led to a deep rivalry and hatred between their sons. Surely, this was not their intent, but nonetheless it did great damage. Jacob flees from his home and is not reunited with his brother until much later in life. The deception and bitterness between the boys robbed them of what could have been a rich relationship.

In looking up the definition of bitterness you'll find two similar but distinct meanings. Both can apply to the believer who falls into its snare:

bitterness—noun

1. Sharpness of taste; lack of sweetness.

2. Anger and disappointment at being treated unfairly; resentment.

It's interesting to me that bitterness is a noun. As I ponder that, it makes me imagine this emotion taking on a life of its own. Or perhaps invading a life where it steals all sweetness and replaces it with anger, disappointment, and resentment as the definition explains.

> **Read Hebrews 12:15 and Ephesians 4:31 (page 57). Circle the command in each verse and then list them in the space below.**

In the Book of Hebrews, we are told to "Watch out . . . ," and in Ephesians we are instructed to "Get rid of. . . ." I like that these are action steps. We have the option to be released from bitterness if we so choose.

When has bitterness affected a relationship in your life?

How did you handle it? How would you handle it differently today if you could?

What work do you need to do "get rid of all bitterness"?

Feeling the love of our parents so deeply as kids left my brothers and me with a deep sense of security. Unfortunately, some of my friends growing up did not have that same experience. They felt that their siblings, or their parents' work, or even the church, took priority over them, and as a result, they had some real feelings of insecurity, bitterness, and resentment. When talking with a college friend recently, I asked about her family, and she said, "Oh, I don't see them much. You know, I was never their favorite." What a painful statement. Her tone was not bitter; it was indifferent. Where hurt once lived, now there was apathy. It made me so sad. She deserves better.

I don't know what your story has been so far. Maybe you have felt that you were not the favorite. If that's the case, and it has been for me at times, then you have felt pain in those relationships. But, let me remind you of the primary narrative of God's big story: You are Chosen! The God of the Universe pursues you because you are precious in His sight. Rest and rejoice in that today.

Prayer

- Ask God to forgive you for when your heart has been bitter.
- Seek to rest in His love as you pray.
- Ask God to help you express His love to others you have struggled to love in the past.

The God of the Universe pursues you because you are precious in His sight.

Day 4

Settle

As you settle into your time with God, just be still and ask God to meet you in these moments. You may want to close your eyes and take a few deep breaths to take in peace and exhale any stress that would distract you during your time with God.

Focus

¹⁴After Jacob had stayed with Laban for about a month, ¹⁵Laban said to him, "You shouldn't work for me without pay just because we are relatives. Tell me how much your wages should be?"

¹⁶Now Laban had two daughters. The older daughter was named Leah, and the younger one was Rachel. ¹⁷There was no sparkle in Leah's eyes, but Rachel had a beautiful figure and a lovely face. ¹⁸Since Jacob was in love with Rachel, he told her father, "I'll work for you for seven years if you'll give me Rachel, your younger daughter, as my wife."

¹⁹"Agreed!" Laban replied. "I'd rather give her to you than to anyone else. Stay and work with me." ²⁰So Jacob worked seven years to pay for Rachel. But his love for her was so strong that it seemed it to him but a few days.

²¹Finally, the time came for him to marry her. "I have fulfilled my agreement," Jacob said to Laban. "Now give me my wife so I can sleep with her."

²²So Laban invited everyone in the neighborhood and prepared a wedding feast. ²³But that night, when it was dark, Laban took Leah to Jacob, and he slept with her. ²⁴(Laban had given Leah a servant, Zilpah, to be her maid.)

²⁵But when Jacob woke up in the morning—it was Leah! "What have you done to me?" Jacob raged at Laban. "I worked seven years for Rachel! Why have you tricked me?"

²⁶"It's not our custom here to marry off a younger daughter ahead of the firstborn," Laban replied. ²⁷"But wait until the bridal week is over; then we'll give you Rachel, too—provided you promise to work another seven more years for me."

²⁸So Jacob agreed to work seven more years. A week after Jacob had married Leah, Laban gave him Rachel, too. ²⁹(Laban gave Rachel a servant, Bilhah, to be her maid.) ³⁰So Jacob slept with Rachel, too, and he loved her much more than Leah. He then stayed and worked for Laban the additional seven years.

(Genesis 29:14-30)

You are a chosen people. You are royal priests, a holy nation, God's very own possession. As a result, you can show others the goodness of God, for he called you out of the darkness into his wonderful light.

(1 Peter 2:9)

Reflect

There were a lot of things I loved about second grade. We experienced overcrowding in our school that year and I was assigned afternoon classes. So, I got to sleep late and go in at noon. That was nice. I also had a precious teacher, Mrs. Anderson. She was a kind encourager and made a point of making each of us feel special. But, there was a downside to second grade too—recess! Playing kickball was fine, relay races were okay, but the days we played Red Rover were brutal. In case you've never played, here's how it works: Two teams line up opposite of each other. Each team forms a chain by holding hands and then calls a player from the opposite team over, where they run forward and attempt to break through the chain.

It's a straightforward game and I enjoyed it—usually. But in my second-grade class we had two students that were known for something that is not too classy to talk about in a women's Bible study, but since I know you guys can handle it I'll tell you: they were booger eaters. Yes, it's gross! I know!

So, when it came time to choose teams, these two classmates were always chosen last. And, because I was a bleeding heart at seven years old, I often volunteered to hold their hands in the Red Rover lineup. When I got to be captain, I would try to choose them early to compensate for all the times they were chosen dead last. The game made me dread going to recess. And for a time, I even dreaded going to school because of the Red Rover dilemma. But as much as I didn't like second grade, I imagine my two booger-eating classmates liked it even less, because they were the ones getting the teasing. They were the ones who were never chosen first.

When have you had the experience of not feeling included? What were the circumstances?

What emotions do you feel as you look back on that situation?

Today in our reading we see that Jacob the deceiver becomes Jacob the deceived. In Genesis 27 Jacob and his mother, Rebekah, take advantage of Isaac's blindness in stealing the blessing that would have gone to Esau. Now, just two chapters later, in Genesis 29, Rebekah's brother, Laban, takes advantage Jacob.

Read Genesis 29:14-30 (pages 62–63).

Who was the deceiver in this story?

How did he deceive?

Who was chosen? How do you think she felt?

Who was not chosen? How do you think she felt?

I have often wondered just how dark it was, that even with a veiled bride, Jacob couldn't tell that this was Leah instead of Rachel. Then I ran across some writings from the church historian Josephus. He suggests that as Isaac is deceived because of physical blindness, Jacob is deceived through drunken blindness. In other words, he was so drunk he didn't even notice which daughter he took home.

Another thing that's important is that the feast wasn't a wedding party. There's no mention of women being there. The Hebrew word used for the wedding party is *mishteh*, which translates as "drinking party." Okay, now this is making sense. I imagine Laban brought out the best wines to orchestrate a scenario where he could trick Jacob and marry off both daughters, requiring seven more years of labor and a lifetime of turmoil for them all.

Lying and deception apparently run in this family line. (And as we will see tomorrow, it continues into the next generation as well!)

What traits—both good and bad—have been passed down in your family?

Which traits would you like to pass on to your children and grandchildren?

> **Recognizing who we are in Christ and knowing that our worth comes from Him, not from the approval of others, can lead us into lives free from bitterness.**

Which ones do you want to stop with you?

How will you do it—pass on the good, and stop the bad?

Like Leah and my friends from the second grade, I have had times in my life when I've known I was not the favorite. I was not the "chosen" one. Sometimes, it didn't matter to me one bit. Other times, it stung a lot! I imagine you have felt that way at times too. With maturity we can learn to be gracious and just move on with our lives. But, sometimes, no matter how hard we try to be mature, it just hurts. And, if we aren't careful, that hurt can turn to bitterness or anger, like it did with Esau and Leah.

Recognizing who we are in Christ and knowing that our worth comes from Him, not from the approval of others, can lead us into lives free from bitterness and the hurt of not feeling chosen. In fact, we can move into a beautiful place of knowing our true worth and living into that value!

Leah may not have been chosen by Jacob, but she was chosen by God. In fact, we read, "When the LORD saw that Leah was unloved, he enabled her to have children" (Genesis 29:31). In fact, of the twelve sons of Jacob, which later become the twelves tribes of Israel, Leah is the mother of six! God saw her. He chose her and He blessed her.

You too are chosen. First Peter 2:9 promises, "You are a chosen people. You are royal priests, a holy nation, God's very own possession. As a result, you can show others the goodness of God, for he called you out of the darkness into his wonderful light."

Remembering who chooses us can give us the peace and strength to face our earthly critics and temporary rejections. *You are chosen.* Let that be like cool water washing over your soul today, refreshing you and reminding whose you are!

Prayer

Listen to "Waymaker," recorded by Passion, or listen to another song of your choice as you pray today. Thank God for all of the ways He chooses you. Ask Him to help you heal and release any bitterness you may be carrying today.

Day 5

Settle

As you pause from today's distractions, do something refreshing. Take a short walk, listen to a song, pet the dog, or something else that brings you joy and lifts your spirit. As you do, enjoy the moment with your Savior.

Focus

³Jacob loved Joseph more than any of his other children because Joseph had been born to him in his old age. So one day Jacob had a special gift made for Joseph—a beautiful robe. ⁴But his brothers hated Joseph because their father loved him more than the rest of them. They couldn't say a kind word to him.

(Genesis 37:3-4)

¹⁸When Joseph's brothers saw him coming, they recognized him in the distance. As he approached, they made plans to kill him. ¹⁹"Here comes the dreamer!" they said. ²⁰"Come on, let's kill him and throw him into one of these cisterns. We can tell our father, 'A wild animal has eaten him'" . . . ²³So when Joseph arrived, his brothers ripped off the beautiful robe he was wearing. ²⁴Then they grabbed him and threw him into the cistern. Now the cistern was empty; there was no water in it. ²⁵Then, just as they were sitting down to eat, they looked up and saw a caravan of camels in the distance coming toward them. . . . ²⁶Judah said to his brothers, "What will we gain by killing our brother? We'd have to cover up the crime. ²⁷Instead of hurting him, let's sell him to those Ishmaelite traders. After all, he is our brother—our own flesh and blood!" And his brothers agreed. . . . ²⁸The traders took him to Egypt.

(Genesis 37:18-19b, 23-28)

¹⁹But Joseph replied, "Don't be afraid of me. Am I God, that I can punish you? ²⁰You intended to harm me, but God intended it all for good. He brought me to

this position so that I could save the lives of many people. [21]*No, don't be afraid. I will continue to take care of you and your children." So he reassured them by speaking kindly to them.*

(Genesis 50:19-21)

We can rejoice, too, when we run into problems and trials, for we know that they help us develop endurance.

(Romans 5:3)

Reflect

Early in ministry, my husband, Jim, and I had several discouraging experiences. There was fruit in each of the ministries, but there were also some critics who made us wary of careers in the local church. What made it worse was that these experiences fell back to back in our lives. As a result, we went through a season when we questioned everything. God, did we miss your calling? What are we doing wrong? Are we on the right track? I remember Jim jokingly saying, "I thought I heard God calling me to the church by name, but maybe he said Tim instead of Jim." We laughed outwardly, but inside we were struggling.

A friend remarked during that time that this was our "character-building season." "Character-building season" is a phrase reserved for times when you feel like you're losing repeatedly. I remember our friend saying, "God must be toughening you guys up for a big work in your future." Maybe so, because one thing was certain: We were not very tough at the time. Every criticism hurt. Every rejection stung. But with each setback, we began to toughen up. Let me let you in on a little secret about character-building seasons: they stink when you're in them! You already know this is if you've ever been through one. And, if you're in one right now, hang on. They don't last forever!

Joseph, eleventh son of Jacob, certainly found himself in season after season of difficulty. Let's learn more about his story.

> **Read Genesis 37:3-4, 18, 23-28 (page 68). Describe the relationship between Joseph and his brothers.**

Why was there such animosity between them?

What do you imagine Joseph was feeling as his brothers sold him into slavery?

Joseph was sold into slavery by his brothers and taken to another country far away from his homeland. To make his situation even worse, his hardship originated from the betrayal of his own brothers. That's a hard pill to swallow. By Genesis 39, though, it seems like things are looking up for Joseph—until they aren't.

Read Genesis 39:1-6a. How did Joseph's situation change?

How do you think Joseph might have felt? In the space below, pretend you are Joseph and write about this experience as if writing in your journal.

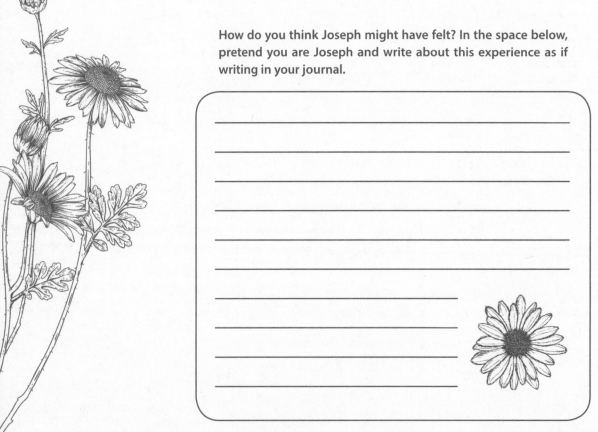

Read Genesis 39:6b-20. How did Joseph's situation change this time?

How do you think Joseph might have felt at this newest turn of events? In the space below, pretend you are Joseph and write about this experience, again as if writing in your journal.

_____

_____

_____

_____

_____

_____

_____

_____

_____

_____

From favored son to Potiphar's slave; falsely accused of rape and sentenced to prison—Joseph's life as favored son must have seemed long behind him. But God is obviously with Joseph through his struggles. Though his trials have been many, Joseph eventually rises to become second-in-command of the nation. (See Genesis 41.) And years after his brothers' betrayal, when reunited with them, Joseph extends grace.

Read Genesis 50:20 (pages 68–69). How does Joseph respond when he meets his brothers face to face?

Joseph redeems the trials he's been through by using what he's learned and the status he has achieved to bring good and not evil. His struggles were not wasted. This is known as redemptive suffering. And like God's passionate pursuit of His people, it is an overarching narrative of Scripture. God specializes in bringing good out of bad.

Read Romans 5:3 (page 69), and rewrite this verse in your own words below.

In what other situations or stories in the Bible can you see God at work in difficult situations? (There are lots of them! Just name a few.)

As I look back on our season of character building, I recognize that some of what we went through was the result of jerks in our journey. Have you ever had any of those? And, some of what we endured was just part of life. But, what I recognize most about those years is that God was with us in the yuck. And the struggle of seeking God in dark moments led us to seek Him with our whole hearts. It also toughened us up so that we could endure other hardships that came our way. Honestly, I don't know if we would be who we are or where we are in life today without the struggles of those early years. What others meant to harm us, God turned to good as we sought Him in those challenges. Those years of suffering were not wasted. God redeemed them through character building.

What difficult seasons have you endured (death of a loved one, disease, job loss, depression, divorce, addiction, betrayal, and so on)?

How are you different because of those experiences?

As you go through your own hard times, remember these two truths:

1. God loves you and passionately pursues you. This is why Jesus came for you.
2. God never wants to waste a hurt. He can turn your greatest suffering into your greatest ministry if you allow it.

   What hurts from your past could you use to minister to others? How?

In Week 1, we explored the love of our Creator God and how He pursued Adam and Eve even after sin entered the picture. This week, we have seen how God chose to start His holy nation through imperfect people. Abraham, Isaac, and Jacob are known as the great patriarchs of the faith. Yet, they were all flawed. So were their wives and children. This is good news for us. We too are flawed. Our stories are messy, but God pursues

If God had a phone, your picture would be His screensaver.

us with a relentless love. If God had a phone, your picture would be His screensaver. You are precious, chosen, and pursued. Allow that to bring you comfort and peace today.

Prayer

- As you pray today, ask God to show you ways that He can take the pain of your past and use it to bless others. How can redemptive suffering be part of your story?
- Thank God for His wisdom and for being with you in the struggles of life.
- Ask God to give you the trust to surrender your current struggles to Him, knowing that He doesn't waste any pain you experience.

Video Viewer Guide
WEEK 2

Scriptures: Genesis 29:14b-21, 25, 30-35, Revelation 3:20

God _____ you.

God _____ you.

God is _____.

Week 3

Pursued in a Cycle of Obedience and Rebellion

JUDGES, KINGS, AND PROPHETS

Day 1

Settle

Take a deep breath, pause and hold it, and then release it slowly. You may want to repeat this a few times to slow your thoughts and allow the stresses of your day to fade away. For these next few moments, give God your full attention and allow Him to speak to you.

Focus

¹As Samuel grew old, he appointed his sons to be judges over Israel. ²Joel and Abijah, his oldest sons, held court in Beersheba. ³But they were not like their father, for they were greedy for money. They accepted bribes and perverted justice.

⁴Finally, all the elders of Israel met at Ramah to discuss the matter with Samuel. ⁵"Look," they told him, "you are now old, and your sons are not like you. Give us a king to judge us like all the other nations have."

⁶Samuel was displeased with their request and went to the Lᴏʀᴅ for guidance. ⁷"Do everything they say to you," the Lᴏʀᴅ replied, "for it is me they are rejecting, not you. They don't want me to be their king any longer. ⁸Ever since I brought them from Egypt they have continually abandoned me and followed other gods. And now they are giving you the same treatment. Do as they ask, but solemnly warn them about the way a king will reign over them."

(1 Samuel 8:1-9)

It is the Lord your God you must follow, and him you must revere. Keep his commands and obey him; serve him and hold fast to him.

(Deuteronomy 13:4 NIV)

Do not conform to the pattern of this world, but be transformed by the renewing of your mind. Then you will be able to test and approve what God's will is—his good, pleasing and perfect will.

(Romans 12:2 NIV)

Reflect

Let's do a big-picture review. In the beginning was perfection. God looked upon all He had made and declared that it was good! Adam and Even dwelled in the Garden of Eden with the Lord and enjoyed a close relationship with Him. But, when they chose their will over God's, sin interrupted that idyllic scenario.

God did not abandon Adam and Eve, but things were different from that point on. Sin grew. In fact, sin became so rampant on earth that by the time of Noah, in Genesis 6, God was sad that He had even created humans—so sad in fact that He sent a flood in order to achieve a reboot. Through the flood, humanity was given another chance to do life God's way. Even in unfaithfulness, God continued to pursue His people and find ways to bring them back into a right relationship with Himself.

After people are reestablished on the earth, God selected a husband-and-wife team, Abraham and Sarah, to be the founders of a new and set-apart nation. Through their lineage we actually trace the roots of the Jewish, Christian, and Muslim faiths today. And, it is from their grandson Jacob, whose name is later changed to Israel, that the Jewish nation is birthed.

In last week's devotional lessons, we left off with Joseph, the son of Jacob (Israel), making a home for his brothers in Egypt. Israel's twelve sons flourish in Egypt. In fact, four hundred years after Joseph and his brothers die, the Israelites are so numerous that the Egyptian rulers are threatened by them and therefore enslave them.

Eventually, God calls one of Israel's descendants, a man named Moses, to lead them out of Egypt and toward the land God promised Abraham long ago—the chosen or Promised Land. This is the area we know as Israel today. Moses does what God calls him to do, and the now-millions of Israelites living in Egypt escape slavery and head toward their new home (the Books of Exodus, Numbers, and Deuteronomy tell this story).

Moses's successor, Joshua, leads them to conquer the land of Israel, and for almost two hundred years, the people of God are led by men and women known as judges. These are people chosen by God to govern spiritually, socially, politically, and militarily. Gideon, Ehud, Deborah, and Samson are among the great judges of the Old Testament. Their stories are found in the Book of Judges.

When the people of Israel stay close to God and His instructions under the judge's leadership, the nation does well. But, when they deviate from God's direction, they fall into trouble (a universal truth for us all, by the way).

The last of the judges is Samuel. During his leadership, the people of Israel took a look around at neighboring countries and decided that they no longer wanted to be led by God and His representatives, the judges. Instead, they wanted what they saw others in the world had—a king. God's people shifted their focus from spiritual to earthly leadership. Let's pick up the story there.

Read 1 Samuel 8:1-9 (page 77).

Describe Samuel's sons, Joel and Abijah.

What do the elders decide when they meet together?

What did Samuel do when he heard the elders' request?

What did God tell Samuel about the elders' request?

Samuel "went to the Lord for guidance" (v. 6) when the people requested a king. They didn't want to see Samuel's sons in the role of judge (probably because they were corrupt!). And they wanted what they saw in other countries—a king. But God made it clear that the real rejection was not of Samuel, the judges, or even his sons. They were ultimately rejecting God's leadership.

When in your lifetime, or in history, have you seen or heard about the church deviating from God's guidance and embracing cultural norms instead?

What practices, habits, or beliefs have you adopted that are culturally acceptable but go against God's standards and commands?

At this point in the biblical narrative, we see a distinct shift from theocracy, which is government through God's appointed leader, to a monarchy, rule by a king or queen. God is clear that this is not what He wants for His people. In fact, He warns them of what is to come if they choose this type of earthly leadership. Here are a few of those warnings and where we see them fulfilled in Scripture:

- drafting sons to military service—fulfilled in 1 Samuel 14:52,
- using slave laborers—fulfilled in 2 Chronicles 2:17-18,
- taking the best of your property and labors—fulfilled in 1 Kings 21:15-16, and
- using your property for the king's purposes—fulfilled in 1 Kings 9:10-14.

Even with God's warnings, the elders of Israel insist on a king. They are afraid of the leadership of Samuel's sons, they want to unite the twelve tribes of Israel, and most of all, they want what the other nations have. They want an earthly king.

When and how have your earthly desires gotten you into trouble?

What brought you back to God's standards? Or if you're still dealing with this issue, what steps can you take today to set things right in God's eyes?

As Israel sought their first king, Saul seemed a good choice. Standing a head taller than other men, handsome, and from a prominent family, he was just the kind of man the elders of Israel were wanting. Though he started off with God's blessings, he soon drifted from God's directions. As he abandoned God's will for his own, Saul became arrogant, impulsive, and jealous.

As the first king of Israel, Saul worked hard to keep up appearances, but he trusted in his own judgment. Instead of seeking God's will, he made his own choices and it caused the nation great trouble. Saul served as king of Israel for the rest of his life, but God made sure that the next king of Israel had a heart more in tune with pleasing Him.

In our theme of being pursued, it is important to note that although the nation rejects God's appointed leaders, the judges, and seeks an earthly king, God does not abandon them. Instead, He gives them the desire of their hearts, an earthly king, and then allows them to reap the

As the Great Pursuer, God stands ready to help you, no matter what you've done or how far you've drifted.

consequences of that choice. But, as a loving Father, He never goes far. And when they get into enough trouble, and they do, they turn back to Him. The great news is as the Great Pursuer, God stands ready to help you, no matter what you've done or how far you've drifted. All you have to do is turn to Him. He is standing there with arms wide open.

Prayer

- Ask God to forgive you when you seek your will over His.
- Confess specific areas of disobedience still present in your life.
- Commit to Him to follow His standards in your life.

Day 2

Settle

Listen to a song that reminds you of your journey into faith today. Maybe a hymn, children's song, or something that brings back the season when you first embraced Jesus as Savior. Let that music remind you of God's overwhelming love for you.

Focus

Now the Lord said to Samuel, "You have mourned long enough for Saul. I have rejected him as king of Israel, so fill your flask with oil and go to Bethlehem. Find a man named Jesse who lives there, for I have selected one of his sons to be my king."

(1 Samuel 16:1)

⁴So Samuel did as the Lord instructed. . . . ⁶When they arrived, Samuel took one look at Eliab and thought, "Surely this is the Lord's anointed!"

⁷But the Lord said to Samuel, "Don't judge by his appearance or height, for I have rejected him. The Lord doesn't see things the way you seem them. People judge by outward appearance, but the Lord looks at the heart."

⁸Then Jesse told his son Abinadab to step forward and walk in front of Samuel. But, Samuel said, "This is not the one the Lord has chosen." ⁹Next Jesse summoned Shimea, but Samuel said, "Neither is this the one the Lord has chosen." ¹⁰In the same way all seven of Jesse's sons were presented to Samuel. But Samuel said to Jesse, "The Lord has not chosen any of these." ¹¹Then Samuel asked, "Are these all the sons you have?"

"There is still the youngest," Jesse replied. "But he's out in the fields watching the sheep and goats."

"Send for him at once," Samuel said. "We will not sit down to eat until he arrives."

¹²So Jesse sent for him. He was dark and handsome, with beautiful eyes.

And the LORD said, "This is the one; anoint him."

(1 Samuel 16:4, 6-12)

²Late one afternoon, after his midday rest, David got out of bed and was walking on the roof of the palace. As he looked out over the city, he noticed a woman of unusual beauty taking a bath. ³He sent someone to find out who she was, and he was told, 'She is Bathsheba, the daughter of Eliam and the wife of Uriah the Hittite.' ⁴Then David sent messengers to get her; and when she came to palace, he slept with her.

(2 Samuel 11:2-4a)

(For more the story of David and Bathsheba, see 2 Samuel 11:5–12:13).

God removed Saul and replaced him with David, a man about whom God said, "I have found David son of Jesse, a man after my own heart. He will do everything I want him to do."

(Acts 13:22)

¹⁰Create in me a clean heart, O God.
Renew a loyal spirit within me.
¹¹Do not banish me from Your presence,
and don't take your Holy Spirit from me.
¹²Restore to me the joy of your salvation,
and make me willing to obey you.

(Psalm 51:10-12)

Reflect

Easter weekends are big events around our household. Some years we have done as many as twelve services from Friday to Sunday. So, as a pastoral family, we know that we need to keep things low-key around the house to help Jim reserve energy and be able to bring the message with equal enthusiasm for each service. So, when we got a call one Easter weekend at 11:00 p.m. on Saturday, it was surprising. Even more surprising was the caller: a sheriff's deputy. He said, "Mrs. Cowart, I'm here with your

son. We just stopped him for speeding. He's seventeen and this will be a super speeder ticket, so we could take him to jail, but instead we're going to let you deal with him. However, you need to know he will lose his license for six months over this."

It was a big event for us. Josh is an easygoing kid and rarely breaks the rules. Having this happen Easter weekend made it even more stressful. But the worst of the whole situation was losing that license for six months. He was duel-enrolled in college and high school classes and playing football, so we had to figure out how to get him from one place to the next every day for six long moths. It was a tough season of life. And for Josh it was embarrassing having to deal with the consequences of having his mom, dad, and friends taxi him around.

However, Josh did not waste this experience. Today, he is an excellent and cautious driver. He leaves in plenty of time to get where he is going and plans his routes in advance. When I think of reckless drivers or poor decision makers, Josh doesn't come to mind. He redeemed his reputation with how repentant he was and how he changed his behavior.

What would you say is the worst thing you've ever done? Dig deep—you may not even be able to bring yourself to write it down.

How would this action continue to affect you if you felt that it defined you on a daily basis?

When we think of David, so many images come to mind: shepherd, poet, musician, king, and ancestor of Jesus. These are all correct, and they are strong and faithful descriptions. But to capture the full picture, there is another list: betrayer, adulterer, murderer, and liar. Scripture makes no attempt to hide David's imperfections. Second Samuel 11 gives us great detail about David's less than righteous actions.

Read 2 Samuel 11:1-5.

How did David and Bathsheba meet?

What does the passage tell us about Bathsheba?

What was the result of David and Bathsheba's encounter?

Read 2 Samuel 11:6-17.

What did David do to cover up his infidelity?

What was the end result of David's actions?

This is a sad story in Scripture. David sees a beautiful woman, desires her, and sleeps with her even though he knows she is married to Uriah. When she becomes pregnant from their encounter, David brings Uriah home from battle in hopes that Uriah will have sex with her. No one would know the child was actually David's. When that plan fails because of Uriah's integrity, David has Uriah killed and takes Bathsheba as his wife.

We see clearly that David is not a perfect man, and although history doesn't forget David's sins, it also does not define him by them.

Read Acts 13:22. How does the writer describe David?

Instead of being known by his greatest failures, David was known as Israel's greatest and most faithful king. How is it that a man who covers his infidelity with murder is described as a man after God's own heart? Usually, when someone messes up this big, their moral collapse follows and defines them forever. But this is not the case with David. Why?

Because he had an unshakable faith and a zeal to know and please God; his attitude was one of devotion and passion to the God He served; and when confronted with his sins, David didn't make excuses. He didn't use his position as king as an excuse. He turned back to God in brokenness and humility. He desperately wanted to renew a right relationship with God.

Read Psalm 51.

What words describe David's approach to God?

Whom did he blame for his sin?

What did David want from God?

What did David promise in return?

Wash me clean. Purify me from my sin. Create in me a clean heart. Renew a loyal spirit within me. Forgive me. These are all phrases poured out to God in this beautiful psalm. What do

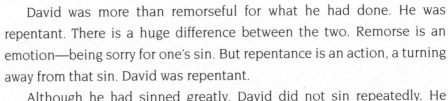
you imagine God might have felt as He heard David repent in this passionate way?

What we do in response to our sin is what shapes our legacy and, more important, our relationship with our heavenly Father.

David was more than remorseful for what he had done. He was repentant. There is a huge difference between the two. Remorse is an emotion—being sorry for one's sin. But repentance is an action, a turning away from that sin. David was repentant.

Although he had sinned greatly, David did not sin repeatedly. He did not establish a pattern of adultery, lying, and infidelity. He sinned, repented, asked for forgiveness, and then lived more righteously.

What we do in response to our sin is what shapes our legacy and, more important, our relationship with our heavenly Father. David learned from his mistakes and made a point not to repeat them in the future. There were consequences to his sin, and he did not want to have to experience that pain again. David also deeply grieved the separation from God that his sins created. What he longed for was to be restored into a right relationship with God.

As a mom, wife, and even as a friend, I try to imagine what I would feel if my children, husband, or close friends had wronged me greatly and then pleaded with me for forgiveness in this way. I could be vengeful, wanting to punish them. I could be hard-hearted, trying to protect myself from being hurt again in the future. I could just be mean and reject them entirely. But if I wanted to express love, I would be faithful to them even when their faithfulness was lacking.

This is what God does for David. Although David is not a perfect child, God is a perfect Father. He chooses David, forgives him, protects, directs and passionately pursues him. In return, David zealously lives and leads in ways that bring honor to God. This repentant heart that is eager to

please God is a huge part of why David is described as a man after God's own heart.

God does the same thing with you and me. Even though we sin, God pursues us and longs for restored relationship. Many times, the only thing keeping us from God is ourselves.

May we have hearts like David's—willing to confront and repent of our sins and then live with passion in ways that honor the God who pursues us!

Prayer

- Today pray back to God David's prayer, making it your own:

> *Create in me a clean heart, O God,*
> *And renew a steadfast spirit within me.*
> *Do not cast me away from Your presence*
> *And do not take Your Holy Spirit from me.*
> *Restore to me the joy of Your salvation*
> *And sustain me with a willing spirit.*
>   (Psalm 51:10-12 NASB)

Day 3

Settle

Start your devotional today with a few deep breaths. As you breathe in, invite the Holy Spirit to do His work in you. As you exhale, release your worries and concerns into God's hands and allow your heart to be at rest.

Focus

> Walk with the wise and become wise, for a companion of fools suffers harm.
> (Proverbs 13:20 NIV)

³Solomon loved the LORD and followed all the decrees of his father, David, except that Solomon, too, offered sacrifices and burned incense at the local places of worship. . . .

⁵That night the LORD appeared to Solomon in a dream, and God said, "What do you want? Ask, and I will give it to you!"

⁶Solomon replied, "You showed faithful love to your servant my father, David, because he was honest and true and faithful to you. And you have continued to show this great and faithful love to him today by giving him a son to sit on his throne.

⁷"Now, O LORD my God, you have made me king instead of my father, David, but I am like a little child who doesn't know his way around. ⁸And here I am in the midst of your own chosen people, a nation so great and numerous they cannot be counted! ⁹Give me an understanding heart so that I can govern your people well and know the difference between right and wrong. For who by himself is able to govern this great people of yours?"

¹⁰The Lord was pleased that Solomon had asked for wisdom. ¹¹So God replied, "Because you have asked for wisdom in governing by people with justice and have not asked for a long life or wealth or the death of your enemies—¹²I will give you what you asked for! I will give you a wise and understanding heart such as no one else has had or ever will have! ¹³And I will also give you what you did not ask for—riches and fame! No other king in all the world will be compared to you for the rest of your life! ¹⁴And if you follow me and obey my decrees and my commands as your father, David, did, I will give you a long life."

(1 Kings 3:3, 5-14)

If any of you lacks wisdom, you should ask God, who gives generously to all without finding fault, and it will be given to you.

(James 1:5 NIV)

Reflect

Intelligence and wisdom are very different things. A person can be very knowledgeable in various areas—travel, technology, culinary arts, astronomy, science, mathematics, even theology—but that will not guarantee wisdom. The good news is God loves and pursues all people, whether or not they are wise. But the benefits of wisdom are much greater than intelligence alone!

While in a meeting recently someone remarked, "Well, as the smartest person in the room I think we should...." First, I frowned; it was insulting to the people in the room, including me! But, then I began to giggle, because the smartest person in the room would never, ever say "As the smartest person in the room...." The truth is this particular individual is very intelligent in several areas. However, interpersonal relationships obviously is not one of them. It was not a wise comment. Not only were his ideas poorly received that day, but the camaraderie of the whole team was damaged.

As followers of Christ it is important that we seek both knowledge and wisdom.

> **Read Proverbs 13:20 (page 90). What reason does this verse give for seeking wisdom?**

These are the words of King Solomon, David's son and one of the authors of Proverbs and possibly of Ecclesiastes and Song of Songs.

At the death of King David, his son Solomon was passed the mantle of leadership. Early in Solomon's reign the Lord spoke to him in a dream and made him an amazing offer.

Read 1 Kings 3:5-14 (pages 90–91). What did God ask Solomon?

What did Solomon request, and what was God's response?

What else did God grant Solomon?

Solomon's answer pleased the Lord, because he asked for wisdom to be able to lead the people of Israel in a way that honored God. In fact, the Lord was so pleased that He not only granted Solomon's wish but also blessed him with riches, fame, and a long life. In fact, 1 Kings 3:10, 11 tells us, "The Lord was pleased that Solomon had asked for wisdom....I will give you what you asked for! I will give you a wise and understanding heart such as no one else has had or ever will have!"

I love this passage! In fact, I often pray what Solomon did: *Oh Lord, please give me wisdom. Help me to see things from your perspective so that I can live in ways that please you. However, I have learned that this prayer only pays off when we both know and do God's will.*

There is a huge disparity between knowing what is wise and doing what is wise. King Solomon is a great example of this. Although, through God's grace, he was the wisest person who had ever lived (1 Kings 4:30), he often did not make wise choices. Instead of pursuing God's purposes for himself and the kingdom, Solomon regularly pursued his own pleasures. For instance, he married foreign women—many of them. And their influence led him astray.

There is a huge disparity between knowing what is wise and doing what is wise.

Read 1 Kings 11:4 in the margin. In what way did Solomon's foreign wives lead him astray? What was the result?

As Solomon grew old, his wives turned his heart after other gods, and his heart was not fully devoted to the Lord his God, as the heart of David his father had been.

(1 Kings 11:4 NIV)

Although King Solomon didn't blow it as badly as King Saul had done, neither did he live into the footsteps of his father, David. Upon his father's death, Solomon inherited a prosperous and thriving kingdom. But shortly after Solomon's death, the kingdom would be divided and never fully reunited. How could the wisest man who had ever lived make so many mistakes?

Knowing God's will and doing God's will have to be in sync! The apostle Paul reflects on this in his Letter to the Romans.

Read Romans 7:15-20 and describe how this applies to your life today:

Although it is debated, some scholars believe Solomon wrote the Book of Ecclesiastes, in which the writer ponders the meaning of life.

Look up the following verses and jot down your thoughts as you consider these instructions:

Ecclesiastes 2:1-11:

Ecclesiastes 7:11-12:

Ecclesiastes 12:1-7:

If Solomon did write Ecclesiastes, he ends the book with perhaps his wisest words of all: "Fear God, and keep his commandments; for that is the whole duty of everyone" (12:13 NRSV). Friend, this is a good word for us today. As we seek Christ, may we seek not only knowledge of what He would have us do but also wisdom for how to do it.

Prayer

- As you pray today, use James 1:5 (NIV) to guide you:

  If any of you lacks wisdom, you should ask God, who gives generously to all without finding fault, and it will be given to you.

  Jesus,

  I need Your wisdom regarding _____

  _____.

  I trust You as my Father who wants to give good gifts to your children (see Matthew 7:11). I know You give generously and you will provide the wisdom I need. Thank You for caring about every detail of my life, including this area. In Jesus's name. Amen.

Day 4

Settle

Set a timer for four minutes and just be still. In your stillness, ask God to speak to your heart and calm your emotions so that you can put all your energy into seeking Him during this precious time together.

Focus

¹Now Elijah, who was from Tishbe in Gilead, told King Ahab, "As surely as the LORD, the God of Israel, lives—the God I serve—there will be no dew or rain during the next few years until I give the word!"

²Then the LORD said to Elijah, ³"Go to the east and hide by the Kerith Brook, near where it enters the Jordan River. ⁴Drink from the brook and eat what the ravens bring you, for I have commanded them to bring you food."

⁵So Elijah did as the LORD told him . . . ⁷for there was no rainfall anywhere in the land.

(1 Kings 17:1-7)

¹Later on, in the third year of the drought, the LORD said to Elijah, "Go and present yourself to King Ahab. Tell him that I will soon send rain!" . . .

¹⁷When Ahab saw him, he exclaimed, "So, is it really you, you troublemaker of Israel?"

¹⁸"I have made no trouble for Israel," Elijah replied. "You and your family are the troublemakers, for you have refused to obey the commands of the LORD and have worshiped the images of Baal instead. ¹⁹Now summon all Israel to join me

at Mount Carmel, along with the 450 prophets of Baal and the 400 prophets of Asherah who are supported by Jezebel."

(1 Kings 18:1, 17-19)

(Read 1 Kings 18:22-45 for the dramatic conclusion of this showdown!)

¹When Ahab got home, he told Jezebel everything Elijah had done, including the way he had killed all the prophets of Baal. ²So Jezebel sent this message to Elijah: "May the gods strike me and even kill me if by this time tomorrow I have not killed you just as you killed them."

³Elijah was afraid and fled for his life. . . . ⁴He sat down under a solitary broom tree and prayed that he might die. "I have had enough, Lord." he said. "Take my life, for I am no better than my ancestors who have already died."

(1 Kings 19:1-4b)

⁹Two are better than one,
     because they have a good return for their labor:
¹⁰If either of them falls down,
     one can help the other up.
But pity anyone who falls
     and has no one to help them up.

(Ecclesiastes 4:9-10 NIV)

Reflect

When the COVID-19 virus was raging in the U.S., my husband and I had just returned from Africa by way of several stops, including New York, and then were isolated for several weeks. Honestly, the first few days were a welcome rest after being evacuated out of Africa. Then we set out to figure out how to do things in new ways. Having groceries delivered to the door and connecting through video technology with our family and staff members took a day or two to master. But once the reality of homebound life had set in, I missed my people. It had become lonely. I noticed that although we didn't want to be in crowds at all, we did crave the companionship and fellowship of those we hold dear.

My friendships with other believers encourage my faith. They make me laugh, hold me accountable, and give me an outlet to share dreams, thoughts, and ideas. They pray with me and for me, and I do the same for them. Life without them is harder and not as much fun.

Who make up your spiritual support system?

How do they affect your life?

How can you express appreciation to them this week?

So far this week, we have explored Old Testament life under the judges, and a few of the early kings of Israel—Saul, David, and Solomon. In addition to the leadership of the kings, Israel was also guided by godly prophets who spoke for the Lord and tried to guide the nation into right living.

Perhaps the most famous prophet of the Old Testament is Elijah. His stories are grand. Among the feats on his spiritual résumé, Elijah single-handedly called down fire from heaven in a showdown against hundreds of pagan priests; he raised the dead; he multiplied olive oil and flour; and perhaps most noteworthy, instead of dying he was escorted to heaven on a chariot of fire. Surely, this man loved God and followed Him closely. Of course, Elijah achieved none of this through his own strength, but through his faith in the One true God.

When Elijah first arrives on the scene in 1 Kings 17, the nation of Israel is in trouble. No longer united, the nation is divided into two kingdoms. The Southern Kingdom is now known as Judah and the northern tribes have aligned as Israel. This northern area had no devout kings during

Elijah's time. Instead, they were wicked men who did not follow God's principles. Ahab, Manassah, Amon—these are just a few of the kings who ruled without fear of the Lord. So, God raised up prophets to speak to the nation and try to rescue the people from the wicked kings. In general, these prophets were not popular, and their messages were not well received. But, they were faithful to relay to God's people His will, His love, and His consequences in times of disobedience.

After three years of drought, Elijah challenges the idolatrous prophets to a confrontation at Mount Carmel.

Read 1 Kings 18:18-38

What challenge did Elijah set forth?

Complete the following chart to dissect the passage:

	Side 1: Ahab	Side 2: Elijah
Deity Served:	_____	_____
Preparation of sacrifice:	_____	_____
Actions of the prophet(s):	_____	_____
Results:	_____	_____

When Elijah calls upon Him, God proves His power in a majestic display, first by consuming water-soaked wood in a fire, and then by restoring the rain just as Elijah has prophesied. Yet Elijah is not met with praise. Instead, Ahab's wife, Queen Jezebel, threatens to kill him. One of the great surprises in this story is that after enduring three years of drought, being fed by birds, enjoying a close relationship with God, and even witnessing a dramatic fire-and-rain display from heaven, the threats of one woman cause Elijah to panic.

Reread 1 Kings 18:36-38. What do you imagine Elijah is feeling as he sees the fire flashing from heaven?

Read 1 Kings 19:3-16.

Describe Elijah's state of mind. What clues do you see in these verses?

What does God do for Elijah?

What did God *not* do to Elijah in this state of mind?

Elijah is scared, depressed, and feels alone in serving and honoring God. Yet God provides for him, not just physically and spiritually, but also relationally.

Read 1 Kings 19:19-21. Whom does God provide as a companion?

How do you think Elijah might have felt in having a ministry partner?

After three decades in ministry, I relate to Elijah's highs and lows. His spiritual bipolar complexity is all too real for me. Perhaps you know this struggle as well. There are times when I feel God's power at work in and

We need people— God's people— around us to help us remember that we are chosen, precious, and pursued— especially in our sad moments.

through me. I see Him moving and I'm excited just to be along for the ride. And then, often without notice, it's lonely. Maybe this a tool Satan uses to discourage us. The loneliness can cause doubts—about ourselves and our worth. If left unabated, doubts can spiral downward for many people, leaving them depressed and afraid—much like Elijah.

We need people like Elisha in our lives—other Christ followers who love the Lord and who can come alongside us, freely speaking into our lives to remind us who and whose we are. We are not meant to do life alone. We all have highs and lows, and we need people—God's people— around us to help us remember that we are chosen, precious, and pursued—especially in our sad moments.

Read Ecclesiastes 4:9-10 (page 96). According to these verses, why do we need one another?

When have you felt alone in your spiritual journey?

When have you been helped by a fellow believer?

Where might you find, or create, a strong spiritual support group?

If the great prophet Elijah experienced times of isolation and loneliness, then we know that we will experience them, too. Taking the time to build a spiritual support system will help us live in the knowledge that we are loved, chosen, and pursued, no matter how we might feel in the moment. It also will allow us to breathe encouragement into the lives of others in the way that Elijah did for Elisha, as we will see tomorrow.

Prayer

- Thank God that He is with you in your highs and lows.
- Praise Him for His unwavering passion for you.
- Call out by name those who have encouraged you in your faith, asking God to pour blessings over their lives.
- Ask God for godly women who will guide, correct, and encourage you as you seek to live for Him.

Day 5

Settle

Take a deep breath and exhale. For the next ten minutes, do something that brings you joy. Ride a bike, sing a song, draw, paint, play with your dog, just creatively relax and enjoy the presence of the Lord.

Focus

¹⁵Then the Lord told him [Elijah], "Go back the same way you came, and travel to the wilderness of Damascus…¹⁶and anoint Elisha son of Shaphat from the town of Abel-meholah to replace you as my prophet…. ¹⁹So Elijah went and found Elisha son of Shaphat plowing a field…Elijah went over to him and threw his cloak across his shoulders and then walked away. ²⁰Elisha left the oxen standing there, [and] ran after Elijah.

(1 Kings 19:15-16,19-20a)

¹When the Lord was about to take Elijah up to heaven in a whirlwind, Elijah and Elisha were traveling from Gilgal. ²And Elijah said to Elisha, "Stay here, for the Lord has told me to go to Bethel."

²But Elisha replied, "As surely as the Lord lives and you yourself live, I will never leave you!" So they went down together to Bethel….

⁹When they came to the other side, Elijah said to Elisha, "Tell me what I can do for you before I am taken away."

And Elisha replied, "Please let me inherit a double share of your spirit and become your successor."

¹⁰"You have asked a difficult thing," Elijah replied. "If you see me when I am taken from you, then you will get your request. But if not, then you won't."

¹¹As they were walking along and talking, suddenly a chariot of fire appeared, drawn by horses of fire. It drove between the two men, separating them, and Elijah was carried by a whirlwind into heaven.

(2 Kings 2:1-2, 9-11)

³Likewise, teach the older women to be reverent in the way they live, not to be slanderers or addicted to much wine, but to teach what is good. ⁴Then they can urge the younger women to love their husbands and children, ⁵to be self-controlled and pure, to be busy at home, to be kind, and to be subject to their husbands, so that no one will malign the word of God.

(Titus 2:3-5 NIV)

Reflect

Do you have any regrets? Surely, we all have some. Things we wish we hadn't said or done, or perhaps missed opportunities to do new things or bless people in precious ways. I try to live my life regret-free, but of course no one can do that completely.

As I look back on my life, one of my regrets is that I didn't seek out ministry role models earlier in life. What a blessing it would have been to have had some godly ministry mentors in my twenties. In my early thirties, a friend advised me to get a ministry coach. He said, "You're wanting to do things you have never seen done before. Go for it, but find some people out there who are a few steps ahead of you and learn from them. Don't try to invent every excellent idea and practice."

That was just good sense. What a great idea! I had actually already employed this tactic in my parenting and marriage by finding women a few steps ahead of me who had done family life well. But in my ministry, how would I do that? Where were these innovative sages of wisdom to be found?

Perhaps you have some people in your life like this; if so, that's awesome. Treasure them! But for me, they weren't right in front of me. I actually had to seek them out. Over the years, I have asked coaches and mentors from all over the world if I could come alongside them to learn.

Their expertise has varied, but what they all have in common is that they made me a better person. My only regret is that I wasn't intentional in surrounding myself with these types of people earlier in life.

Who has been a mentor for you?

In which areas of your life could you use a coach right now?

Where could you begin to search for that expertise and friendship?

As we saw yesterday, after the great victory at Mount Carmel, Ahab and Jezebel vow to kill Elijah. This leaves him feeling isolated and lonely. He needed companionship. Elisha, on the other hand, needed a mentor. Someone who could come alongside him as an instructor to help mold him into the prophet God wanted him to be. Their partnership was a blessing for them both.

Read 2 Kings 2:1-2, 9-11. What do these verses tell us about this friendship?

God, in His passionate pursuit, knew what each of these men needed, and was gracious to meet those needs by bringing them together.

Read 1 Kings 19:15-16.

What did God tell Elijah to do?

Why did God tell Elijah to backtrack?

Notice that it was not an accident that their paths crossed, God specifically sends Elijah to find Elisha and anoint him (1 Kings 19:15). God was critically involved in developing this special relationship.

There are times when I have felt alone in my spiritual journey like Elijah. I'll bet you have too. As a woman who is being relentlessly pursued by your heavenly Father, you can be assured that God wants you to have strong, faithful relationships. God plays a part in this and you have a role to play. When Elijah placed his cloak around Elisha's shoulders, Elisha could have shrugged it off, but he didn't. Scripture says Elisha ran after Elijah. He ran after the opportunity to learn from a godly mentor.

This is a lesson we need today! We need to ask God to surround us with mature believers from whom we can learn. We need to be aware that there are those out there who need to learn from us. And we need to run to these opportunities.

Read Titus 2:3-5. How can you put this passage into action?

I once heard an older man speaking to my son, Josh, who was only eight at the time, and he said, "Young man, I look forward to seeing what you will do with your life, for you will be standing on the shoulders of your father." It was a heavy comment for a little boy. Josh had no idea what that meant; he hadn't literally stood on his dad's shoulders for years. I doubt Josh has thought about it since. On the other hand, I think of it often. This wise gentleman was right. We all stand on the shoulders of those who have gone before us and on those from whom we have learned life lessons. So, as we are able, we should choose those people carefully.

And as we mature, we should return the favor by allowing others to stand on our shoulders. Sharing the wisdom we have learned from the

> **Our pouring into other people—and their pouring into us—is another way in which God pursues His children.**

Lord, His Word, and from our own mistakes is a valuable gift to the next generation. Our pouring into other people—and their pouring into us—is another way in which God pursues His children.

> **How can you serve others as a mentor? What strengths of character or skills do you have that you could share with the next generation?**

Elisha needed a mentor, and Elijah needed a mentee. It's interesting to note that while Elijah did amazing miracles, fourteen of which are recorded in the Old Testament, his student Elisha goes on to perform twenty-eight miracles.[4] Twice as many—a double portion. There's no doubt in my mind that Elisha's ministry success is a result of God's favor, his own faith, and the skills he learned from his wise mentor, Elijah.

This week, our focus has been on a few of the judges, kings, and prophets of the Old Testament. Their stories are unique. The time frame spans hundreds of years. But what they have in common is that the God of the universe was passionate in wanting a relationship with each of them. God also wanted a relationship with His people, and he used these leaders to help guide the spiritual direction in the land. We also see that as they drift from Him, as humans often do, God is quick to respond when they turn their hearts back to Him. They are pursued—relentlessly! And, dear friend, so are you!

Prayer

- As you pray today, ask God to surround you with godly people to love and guide you closer to Him and His will for your life.
- Thank God for those He has already sent and ask Him to reveal to you how you can reach out to mentor others in their faith as well.

Video Viewer Guide
WEEK 3

Scriptures: Hosea 1:2, Hosea 3:1-3, James 4:4a

We are to offer unconditional _____ and _____.

We are to do what God _____.

We must be fully _____ to God.

God pursues us despite our massive _____.

Pursued and Rescued

JESUS

Day 1

Settle

Start the week strong! Quietly ask God to give you a renewed passion for what lies ahead. Choose to face this week with joy and enthusiasm. Give God your agenda for the week. Allow yourself to be interrupted in order to love people well.

Focus

¹Now the tax collectors and sinners were all gathering around to hear Jesus. ²But the Pharisees and the teachers of the law muttered, "This man welcomes sinners and eats with them."

³Then Jesus told them this parable: ⁴"Suppose one of you has a hundred sheep and loses one of them. Doesn't he leave the ninety-nine in the open country and go after the lost sheep until he finds it? ⁵And when he finds it, he joyfully puts it on his shoulders ⁶and goes home. Then he calls his friends and neighbors together and says, 'Rejoice with me; I have found my lost sheep.' ⁷I tell you that in the same way there will be more rejoicing in heaven over one sinner who repents than over ninety-nine righteous persons who do not need to repent.

⁸"Or suppose a woman has ten silver coins and loses one. Doesn't she light a lamp, sweep the house and search carefully until she finds it? ⁹And when she finds it, she calls her friends and neighbors together and says, 'Rejoice with me; I have found my lost coin.' ¹⁰In the same way, I tell you, there is rejoicing in the presence of the angels of God over one sinner who repents."

¹¹Jesus continued: "There was a man who had two sons. ¹²The younger one said to his father, 'Father, give me my share of the estate.' So he divided his property between them.

¹³"Not long after that, the younger son got together all he had, set off for a distant country and there squandered his wealth in wild living. ¹⁴After he had spent everything, there was a severe famine in that whole country, and he began to be in need. ¹⁵So he went and hired himself out to a citizen of that

country, who sent him to his fields to feed pigs. [16]He longed to fill his stomach with the pods that the pigs were eating, but no one gave him anything.

[17]"When he came to his senses, he said, 'How many of my father's hired servants have food to spare, and here I am starving to death! [18]I will set out and go back to my father and say to him: Father, I have sinned against heaven and against you. [19]I am no longer worthy to be called your son; make me like one of your hired servants.' [20]So he got up and went to his father.

"But while he was still a long way off, his father saw him and was filled with compassion for him; he ran to his son, threw his arms around him and kissed him.

[21]"The son said to him, 'Father, I have sinned against heaven and against you. I am no longer worthy to be called your son.'

[22]"But the father said to his servants, 'Quick! Bring the best robe and put it on him. Put a ring on his finger and sandals on his feet. [23]Bring the fattened calf and kill it. Let's have a feast and celebrate. [24]For this son of mine was dead and is alive again; he was lost and is found.' So they began to celebrate.

[25]"Meanwhile, the older son was in the field. When he came near the house, he heard music and dancing. [26]So he called one of the servants and asked him what was going on. [27]'Your brother has come,' he replied, 'and your father has killed the fattened calf because he has him back safe and sound.'

[28]"The older brother became angry and refused to go in. So his father went out and pleaded with him. [29]But he answered his father, 'Look! All these years I've been slaving for you and never disobeyed your orders. Yet you never gave me even a young goat so I could celebrate with my friends. [30]But when this son of yours who has squandered your property with prostitutes comes home, you kill the fattened calf for him!'

[31]"'My son,' the father said, 'you are always with me, and everything I have is yours. [32]But we had to celebrate and be glad, because this brother of yours was dead and is alive again; he was lost and is found.'"

(Luke 15:1-32)

For God made Christ, who never sinned, to be the offering for our sin, so that we could be made right with God through Christ.

(2 Corinthians 5:21)

⁶You see, at just the right time, when we were still powerless, Christ died for the ungodly. ⁷Very rarely will anyone die for a righteous person, though for a good man someone might dare to die. ⁸But God demonstrates his own love for us in this: While we were still sinners, Christ died for us.

(Romans 5:6-8 NIV)

Reflect

While at a theme park, I spotted a mom in panic mode. She didn't have to tell me what was wrong. Her face told the story: her child was lost! My mama bear instinct kicked in. People all around us began to join her mission. People began to take action and said, *Show us a picture. Alert security. We'll all stop what we're doing. The rides can wait. We'll help. We have to find the one who is lost*!

Have you ever had that experience? If so, you already know that when someone you love is lost, it is terrifying! Everything else stops and your entire focus becomes a rescue mission.

When my daughter was an infant, she rolled for the first time while I stepped out of the room. She rolled so far, in fact, that she ended up under a table skirt. When I came back into the room two minutes later, she was not in sight. I panicked. Running from room to room my mind was spinning. What could possibly have happened? Did someone take her? Where is she?

In both of these situations, fears were relieved within minutes as the children were found. But not every story ends so well. Sometimes that which is lost is never found, and that is tragic.

> **Recall a time when something precious to you was lost. How did you feel?**

If you are a Christ-follower, recall when you first made a decision to follow Christ. How has that decision changed the trajectory of your life?

In Luke 15, the crowd that assembles around Jesus is diverse. The Pharisees and teachers were there, as we might expect. But as Scripture reveals, also present are tax collectors and notorious sinners. Their presence seems to annoy the church folks. They began to gossip and grumble about Jesus spending time with the riffraff and even sharing meals with them. It's this attitude that triggers Jesus to tell these stories. It's a teachable moment that Jesus seizes to emphasize God's love for all people.

The lost sheep, coin, and sons of Luke 15 are among the best-known parables in Scripture. They illustrate beautifully the lengths God will go to in order to rescue those who are lost.

When have you felt lost or separated from God? What brought you back?

This week as we consider how God relentlessly pursues us, we will focus on the ultimate way this is expressed—through the life, death, and resurrection of Jesus. Jesus came to lead the search for those who are lost. In Week 6, we will spend time considering our role in reaching those around us with God's love, but this week let's keep it close to home. Because sometimes the one who is lost is us!

Read Luke 15:1-31 and complete the chart below.
(*Hint: Two things are lost in verses 11-31.*)

	What was lost?	Who was looking?	What happened when the lost item was found?
vv. 3-7			
vv. 8-10			
vv. 11-31			

Growing up in church, the parables of Luke are overly familiar to me. I can recall pictures from my childhood Bible of a flock of sheep with one little lamb lost over on a hillside. The emphasis in these stories was always on that one sheep separated from the flock, so it surprised me a few years ago when I read Luke 15 again and saw myself in the story. I had always read the story of the sheep and thought, *Okay, cool story. Jesus really loves people far from Him. He even goes after them. He loves them so much. But, I am a church kid. I grew up in Sunday school, youth group, the whole deal. So I guess I'm just one of the ninety-nine.*

As I was reading this story again that day, God spoke to my heart and said, No ma'am, you are not number seventy-four out of ninety-nine. You are the One. You are the One I would look high and low for. You are the One Jesus went to the cross for. You are the One, Jennifer, and so is every person you will ever meet. This revelation was an emotional moment for me. I am not just a number in the church crowd. I am the One, and so are you!

We are the reason Jesus came to earth on a rescue mission.

"The Son of Man came to seek and to save the lost."
(Luke 19:10 NIV)

For the wages of sin is death, but the free gift of God is eternal life in Christ Jesus our Lord
(Romans 6:23)

We are the reason Jesus came to earth on a rescue mission.

As we saw the first week, our sins condemn us. They cause a break in the relationship we have with God. Jesus solves this dilemma for us through His sacrifice at the cross. There is mystery in this atonement process. If I were God, I would have wanted another method of redemption—something, anything, that didn't involve sacrificing my only son. But God in His wisdom knows best. Through Jesus we have the opportunity for eternal life!

Read the Scriptures in the margin and then write below what these mean for you personally (how they apply to your life).

Luke 19:10:

Romans 6:23:

Place yourself in the crowd with Jesus the day He shares these stories. Allow the celebrative spirit in these parables to become part of your story. When the sheep, coin, and son are recovered, a party breaks out because that which is lost is found. God celebrates you! Like a parent celebrates and is relieved when a lost child comes home, your heavenly Father rejoices over you.

Prayer

Lift up to the Lord today prayers of thanks for His relentless pursuit to bring you into right standing with God. And begin to pray for those close to you who do not yet have a relationship with Him.

Day 2

Settle

Take out a notepad and write down today's to-do list (if you haven't already). Now put all of that aside for these moments. Ask God to clear your mind as you focus solely on Him. Allow His agenda for your day to become your agenda today. When you pick your list up after your time with Him today, it just may be that He reprioritizes that list.

Focus

I stand silently before the Lord, waiting for him to rescue me. For salvation comes from him alone.

(Psalm 62:1 TLB)

There's no such thing as self-rescue,
 pulling yourself up by your bootstraps.
The cost of rescue is beyond our means.
  (Psalm 49:7-8a The Message)

For the joy set before him he [Jesus] endured the cross, scorning its shame, and sat down at the right hand of the throne of God.

(Hebrews 12:2b NIV)

[16]For God so loved the world that he gave his one and only Son, that whoever believes in him shall not perish but have eternal life. [17]For God did not send his Son into the world to condemn the world, but to save the world through him.

(John 3:16-17 NIV)

Reflect

At the ripe old age of twenty-one, I took a position in an inner-city mission. My responsibilities included the children's afterschool program and crisis intervention counseling. It was a tough gig. Each day was like a made-for-television movie. Our regular clients were prostitutes ready to come off the streets, people in crises due to illness or job loss, and homeless friends in need of a hot meal. My major responsibility was the street children of the neighborhood. Many of them were turned out of their homes to wander during the day and weren't allowed to come home until the streetlights came on at night. I spent my afternoons providing activities and Christian education for those precious kids.

One summer, wanting to provide a special treat for the children, I arranged to take them swimming. This was a new experience for most of them. When we arrived at the pool we asked each child individually, "Can you swim?" A bunch of them admitted right away, "No, I've never even been to a pool or lake before." Okay, shallow end with the lifeguard for them. But several of the kids said, "Oh yeah, I swim all the time." They dove right in.

I decided to keep my eyes on the deep end and noticed right away that one little fella, full of confidence, jumped in and went straight to the bottom. I watched and watched. I began to ask myself, *Is he holding his breath? Is he playing a joke on me? Nope, this kid can't swim and he's about to drown!* So, of course, I dove in (still in my clothes) and tried to pull him out of the water. But, he began to struggle and he fought against me for a few seconds before finally giving up and allowing me to pull him to safety.

As we both lay panting on the side of the pool, I had several statements and questions for this guy. First: "I thought you said you could swim." To which he said, "Well, I take a bath every night and I've never had a problem." He had not realized that the amount and depth of water would make a difference. Second: "Why did you fight me when I got to you?" He said, "I really just wanted to save myself. I didn't want any help."

Thankfully, we had no more dramatic incidents at the pool that day. And, from that time on, we had a mandatory swimming test in the shallow end before anyone entered the water.

As I reflect on that day, I often think about how stubborn we can be in receiving help from others, especially God. In wanting to save ourselves and control our own circumstances, we may often fight against the very One who wants to and has the power to rescue us.

> When have you struggled to solve a problem on your own, only to find that once you released it to God, He was there waiting to rescue you? Describe it briefly:

> What lessons did you learn in that situation?

Earlier in our study we focused on David, one of Israel's greatest kings. He was powerful, wealthy, and a gifted leader. During his reign, he commanded armies and at his word, the nation of Israel responded. Yet David knew there were limits to his power. He recognized his need for a Savior.

> Read Psalm 62:1 (page 115). If you had written this psalm, what would you have said? Write your own paraphrase of this verse.

In wanting to save ourselves and control our own circumstances, we may often fight against the very One who wants to and has the power to rescue us.

No matter how successful we may be, we can't earn, buy, or work our way into heaven. Church membership doesn't save us. Singing in the choir won't do it. Even volunteering in the nursery won't rescue us from our sins. Our only hope is to put our faith in Jesus.

Read Psalm 49:7-8a (page 115).

What are some ways that people try to pull themselves up by their own bootstraps?

What did David mean when he said the price of rescue is too steep?

God knew we were drowning in our own sins. Humanity needed a Savior. This is why Jesus came to earth. He came on a rescue mission. If there had been another way for us to be made right with God, surely Jesus would not have had to take on human flesh and endure the cross. But Scripture tells us that He willingly did this so that we could be saved.

Read Hebrews 12:2b (page 115). What was the source of the joy set before Jesus?

Jesus did not find joy in the cross, but He could look beyond its horror to the end result: restored relationship between God and humanity. God pursues you so passionately that He did not spare even His own Son in the rescue mission to reach you. That, friends, is sacrificial love. If you didn't need a Savior, Jesus would not have come. But He did. Make that truth personal today!

So many people live their lives like my little friend at the pool— struggling for life. But we needn't struggle. Instead, we just need to surrender to the One who pursues us at all costs. The One God sent to rescue us—our Savior, Jesus.

Prayer

As we close today, use your time of prayer to commit or recommit your life to God. Ask God to forgive your sins and dedicate your life to the One who came on a rescue mission for you! Claim the blessings that are yours when you surrender control of your life to Him. He pursues you at great cost. So, quit struggling on your own and allow Him to scoop you up into His arms and rescue you.

Day 3

Settle

Just to mix things up a bit, try a new place to have your time with God today. If weather permits, choose a quiet place outside where you can appreciate God's creation. If you're inside, even a different chair or room can help create a fresh experience. Once you find today's spot, be still a few minutes and allow God to refresh your soul.

Focus

"Though the mountains be shaken
and the hills be removed,
yet my unfailing love for you will not be shaken
nor my covenant of peace be removed,"
says the Lord, who has compassion on you.
(Isaiah 54:10 NIV)

See what great love the Father has lavished on us, that we should be called the children of God! And that is what we are!

(1 John 3:1 NIV)

Dear friends, let us love one another, for love comes from God.
(1 John 4:7a NIV)

[9]This is how God showed his love among us: He sent his one and only Son into the world that we might live through him. [10]This is love: not that we loved God,

but that he loved us and sent his Son as an atoning sacrifice for our sins. [11]*Dear friends, since God so loved us, we also out to love one another.*

(1 John 4:9-11 NIV)

We love because he first loved us.

(1 John 4:19 NIV)

Reflect

Have you noticed how easy it is to like someone once you know that person likes you? In elementary school, for instance, kids often slip one another notes that say "I like you. Do you like me? Circle yes or no." The kid who circles yes is much more likely to make a new friend than the one who responds with a no because we tend to respond in love when we feel loved first.

Even as adults we experience this. While talking to a friend recently, she mentioned a casual acquaintance of mine and remarked, "You know she just loves you. You ought to hear her talk about you. It's precious!" This was new information to me. I barely knew this gal, but I noticed that the next time I saw this acquaintance, I felt close to her. Knowing that she liked and approved of me created a soft spot in my heart for her. I guess it's just human nature. When we feel loved we return it. Most of us operate this way whether we realize it or not.

On the other hand, when you get the impression that someone isn't too crazy about you, you may put up barriers or even find ways to criticize them. Not only do we do this with people, but sometimes we also do this with our heavenly Father.

The intricacies of God's nature are complex, but the message of how He feels about you is not. It's simple: you are loved. Passionately, relentlessly, in a way that may make no sense at all. God loves you! Scriptures promise us that again and again.

> **Read Isaiah 54:10 and 1 John 3:1 (page 120). At the top of the next page, rewrite these passages in your own words as a love letter from God to you.**

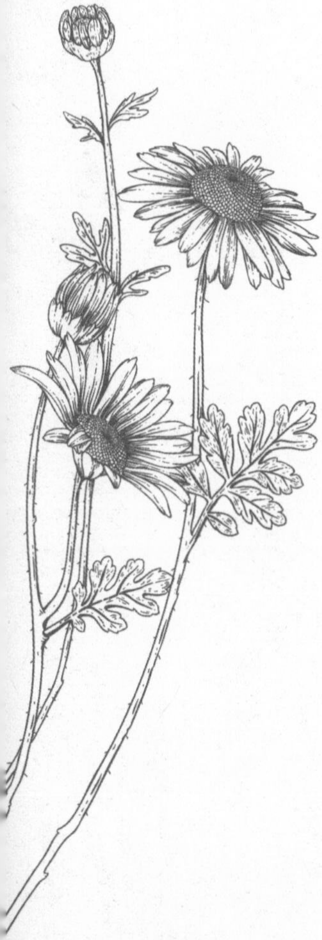

_____

_____

_____

_____

_____

_____

_____

_____

_____

_____

_____

_____

God's ultimate expression of love for us is Jesus. First John 4:9-10 so beautifully states, "This is how God showed his love among us: He sent his one and only Son into the world that we might live through him. This is love: not that we loved God, but that he loved us and sent his Son as an atoning sacrifice for our sins" (NIV).

I once heard my husband say, "Most people's problem is not that they don't love God enough. Their problem is that they don't understand how deeply God loves them. If they understood that, the rest would fall into place." I think there is great wisdom in that.

Far too many people have a distorted image of God. Perhaps, they see Him as an unpleasant parent or strict disciplinarian just waiting to pounce. This faulty image may lead them to distance themselves from

God and His purpose for their lives. But when we understand the depth of God's love for us, everything shifts.

Friend, God chooses you! He pursues you, not because you are good enough or because of anything you have done. God chooses you simply because you are His child. Let that sink in. You are loved and chosen. You are part of His family. This should affect your self-image in the most positive of ways.

God chooses you simply because you are His child.

In 1 John 3:1 (NIV) the apostle writes, "See what great love the Father has lavished on us, that we should be called children of God! And that is what we are!"

What has your image of God been in the past? How does it compare to the description of God in this verse?

Consider traits that a good parent would have toward his or her children. List them here.

Now consider how these traits apply to how God pursues you.

Like you, I love my friends and family, my church members, my small group, and coworkers. These are all precious people in my life. But, when I think about how I love my kids—Josh, Alyssa, and Drew—well that's next-level stuff! So, when the apostle John tells us that it is an honor that God loves us enough to call us His children, I get that!

There is nothing my kids could ever do that would destroy my love for them. Have I been disappointed with them? Yes. Aggravated? Yes. Have I had to discipline them? Yes. But, none of that has ever dampened my love for them. My love for them is ridiculously passionate and always will be. And that's minor stuff in comparison to God's love for you!

Shortly after my daughter married, I hugged my new son-in-law and said, "Son, I love you." I wanted Drew to know that he is part of the family now. It was my way of saying, "You're in! You are chosen—not just by our daughter, but by us, too." There is comfort and security in knowing that we are chosen. This is the comfort God wants you to have as His child.

Once you are secure in knowing that God loves you, that He likes you and chooses you, it will be much easier for you to love those around you. And, once you understand how deeply God loves you, you will tend be more loving and patient with those around you.

First John 4:19 (NIV) says, "We love because he first loved us." God's ultimate expression of love to us is the sacrifice of His Son, Jesus. A Father who would not spare even His Own Son chooses to circle "Yes, I like you" on the note and gives us the freedom not only to love Him in return but also to love those around us. So, today, friend, circle yes—yes, I'll love the people around me because God first loved me!

Pray

Psalm 118:29 says, "Give thanks to the Lord, for he is good; his love endures forever" (NIV). As you pray today, give thanks to the Lord for His love that endures forever. Thank Him for the many ways He expresses His love to you.

Day 4

Settle

Think of a favorite love song, like Elvis's "Love Me Tender," Whitney Houston's "I Will Always Love You," or "When I Fall in Love" by Nat King Cole. Listen to the words and let them be God's love story to you today.

Focus

[1]*"Don't let your hearts be troubled. Trust in God, and trust also in me.* [2]*There is more than enough room in my Father's home. If this were not so, would I have told you that I am going to prepare a place for you?* [3]*When everything is ready, I will come and get you, so that you will always be with me where I am."*

(John 14:1-3)

[25]*Husbands, love your wives, as Christ loved the church and gave himself up for her,* [26]*that he might sanctify her, having cleansed her by the washing of water with the word,* [27]*so that he might present the church to himself in splendor, without spot or wrinkle or any such thing, that she might be holy and without blemish.*

(Ephesians 5:25-27 ESV)

Reflect

Last Christmas I stumbled upon the Hallmark Channel. It was a rainy Saturday and I settled in to check out what I thought would be a predictable, sappy love story. About thirty minutes into the show my son Josh, a college junior, plopped down on the couch next to me and we finished watching together. Neither of us said much. As predicted, there was a happy ending, and as predicted, another show followed immediately.

New small town, different names, same story line. We passed almost four hours that Saturday snuggled up under blankets. I loved it!

At the end of the second movie, we laughed at each other and my son said, "I'm not sure why I kept watching. This is definitely not my kind of show." He's typically an action-adventure kind of guy. Then he said, "Knowing that in the course of two hours there will be a happily ever after with minimal drama and no nasty stuff is a nice emotional break."

Maybe that's the appeal to me too. These fictional movies provide an escape into a nice, neat reality where we know that everything will end well. I've noticed recently that on my most stressful days, I often turn to either HGTV or Hallmark Channel as I wind down my day. In both cases, in a short amount of time something that was a mess is transformed into a beautiful new creation. I like that.

If only life were always that easy. Let me take you back a few thousand years to love stories of the ancient Middle East, where marriages did not unfold like a modern romantic comedy. Romance, and even personal preference, weren't usually taken into consideration. In fact, the bride and groom often had no say in the whole marital transaction. Seriously, this is not Hallmark Channel material. The marriage process seems very foreign by our standards. But, during Jesus's day, this was the normal practice.

Here's how it would usually happen: The bride's and groom's fathers would negotiate an arrangement to wed their children. They would agree upon a bride-price to be paid by the groom's family. Essentially, this bride-price was a transaction that purchased the bride away from her family and brought her into the groom's. These plans were often made during the early years of the bride's and groom's life.

Once the marriage was secured, the fathers often toasted with a glass of wine, and then went home and waited until the children were of age for the next stage of the marriage process: the betrothal.

The betrothal, which we would associate with a time of engagement, was initiated through a ceremony in which the couple came together, sometimes meeting for the very first time, and entered into a legally binding relationship. The betrothal was a serious commitment and could only be ended through divorce. When the betrothal ceremony was over,

the wife went home with her family and the groom with his. It seems odd by our standards, but this couple was now committed to each other for life.

During this time, the groom would work to build another room onto his parents' home to provide a place for him and his bride. Instead of establishing a separate household like we do today, the usual custom was for the groom's family to take the bride into their own home and accept her as family. It would usually take the groom about a year to complete the home addition. Once complete, and without her knowing the day or time, he would go to collect the bride. Her role was to always be ready for her bridegroom's return and to go to her new home.

The betrothal process doesn't sound like romance as we know it today, but it was a beautiful process honored for hundreds of years. It represented dedication, love, and commitment. The faithful bridegroom went ahead of his wife to prepare a permanent home for her. When the time was right, he went to bring her home, where he promised to care for her and make her part of his family forevermore.

This is the context in which the people of Jesus's audience were living. So, when He tells them in John 14 that He is going to prepare a room for them, it is familiar language.

Read John 14:1-3 (page 125). In the space below, write down the actions Jesus promises to take on your behalf.

What does Jesus ask you to do? (verse 1)

He is telling His followers that He has chosen them, that He is committed to them, and that He will go ahead of them to prepare a permanent home where they can dwell as His bride forevermore. This

Jesus does the work necessary to build, to bridge, to repair, and to redeem that which He pursues.

is a beautiful representation of Jesus pursuing us, preparing for us, and providing for us as His beloved.

Ephesians 5:25-27 is a familiar passage often used to define the love between husbands and wives. Today, however, read these verses (page 125) with fresh eyes, paying attention to the role of Jesus and all that He has done for us.

How does Paul describe the relationship between Christ and the church?

How does Paul describe the condition of the church after He sanctifies it?

Think about the level of intimacy between husband and wife. How do you feel as you think about that level of intimacy in your relationship with Jesus?

Over the years, I found that the innocent romance story is fun and has its place, but I'll take dedication and enduring love over fictional story-book romance any day. What Jesus offers His bride is a relentless, unending, ferocious love. Jesus does the work necessary to build, to bridge, to repair, and to redeem that which He pursues. And dear friend, that is you!

Prayer

As a means of prayer, listen to "Ever Be" by Kalley or just read the lyrics online. Allow the words to be your prayer to the bridegroom who has gone to prepare a home for you and will return again for you one day.

Day 5

Settle

Listen, sing, or hum the classic hymn "Blessed Assurance." Reflect on these words and make them your song of praise today:

Blessed assurance, Jesus is mine!
O what a foretaste of glory divine!
Heir of salvation, purchase of God,
born of his Spirit, washed in his blood.

This is my story, this is my song,
praising my Savior all the day long;
this is my story, this is my song,
praising my Savior all the day long.

Perfect submission, all is at rest;
I in my Savior am happy and blest,
watching and waiting, looking above,
filled with his goodness, lost in his love.

Focus

³¹*What, then, shall we say in response to these things? If God is for us, who can be against us?* ³²*He who did not spare his own Son, but gave him up for us all—how will he not also, along with him, graciously give us all things?* ³³*Who will bring any charge against those whom God has chosen? It is God who justifies.* ³⁴*Who then is the one who condemns? No one. Christ Jesus who died—more than that,*

who was raised to life—is at the right hand of God and is also interceding for us. ³⁵Who shall separate us from the love of Christ? Shall trouble or hardship or persecution or famine or nakedness or danger or sword? ³⁶As it is written:

"For your sake we face death all day long;
 we are considered as sheep to be slaughtered."

³⁷No, in all these things we are more than conquerors through him who loved us. ³⁸For I am convinced that neither death nor life, neither angels nor demons, neither the present nor the future, nor any powers, ³⁹neither height nor depth, nor anything else in all creation, will be able to separate us from the love of God that is in Christ Jesus our Lord.

(Romans 8:31-39 NIV)

My dear children, I write this to you so that you will not sin. But if anybody does sin, we have an advocate with the Father—Jesus Christ, the Righteous One.

(1 John 2:1 NIV)

Reflect

What do you think heaven will be like? Scripture gives us glimpses of the beauty and majesty of our eternal home. Streets of gold, rivers like crystals, no sadness, no sickness, worship and joy are the norm. I like to think that the children I lost through miscarriage will meet me soon upon arrival, that Jesus will be there to embrace me, and that others I have loved will be close at hand. There is so much we could ponder, but when I think of heaven, the thing I consider most often is how overwhelming it will be to stand before God. I read the description of heaven in Revelation and the throne of God is intimidating. Honestly, at times it scares me. Who am I to be in the presence of the Creator of the universe?

Now, I've loved the Lord since I was a teenager, worked in vocational ministry, and tried to do good deeds, but I am very much aware of the fact that I am a sinner. My heart and God's Word tell me that I am forgiven, but my head reminds me of the depth of my brokenness. How can someone like me, or any of us for that matter, stand before the Lord God Almighty?

How do you imagine the moment when you will stand before God face to face? Draw a picture of it. Don't worry about whether or not you are a Picasso!

When I think of that moment, I wonder if it may unfold like this:

My head is downcast, partially because of the brilliance of being in God's presence, but also because I can't bear the weight of my own sin. I have faith, but it doesn't feel sufficient. I am scared. To be fully exposed before the One who knows all there is to know of my heart is more than I can handle. The seconds tick by and I fall to my knees before Him. Then the One beside me lifts me to my feet and takes me by the hand.

From the throne before me I hear a booming voice, and the words echo, "This one is not worthy." Heaven is a perfect place, and even as hard as I've tried, I don't fit that description. The gentle but strong voice of Jesus speaks, "No, Father, on her own she is not worthy, but Jennifer is with Me. I have paid the price for her sin." And then through some miraculous heavenly occurrence, I am fully aware of what has been done for me: I am washed clean. Not only is the stain of my sins gone, but even I cannot recall them. No guilt, just joy remains. And in a pure moment, I turn and jump into the arms of the One who has interceded for me: my Savior, my friend, my pursuer—Jesus.

I know it's my imagination, but can you go there with me? Can you make this sentence personal? Write your name in the space below and read it several times aloud. Then record your emotions.

No, Father, on her own she is not worthy, but

_____

is with me. I have paid the price for her sin.

My emotions:

When have you needed someone to speak up for you, to defend you? Was anyone there for you? How did you feel in that situation?

This is the glorious news and the truth from God's Word: Because of Christ, you stand forgiven. The only One who could condemn you has given His life for you.

Read Romans 8:31-39 (pages 129–130). In the space at the top of the following page, list the questions Paul asked in these verses. Then, write the answers you would give in response.

Questions	Answers
v. 31	
v. 32	
v. 33	
v. 34	
v. 35	

Yet Jesus called him. What a shock that must have been to those in the crowd. Even the disciples must have murmured. But, surely the one most shocked must have been Matthew himself. He presents us to God as holy and blameless (Ephesians 5:27). In fact, He serves as an advocate.

Read 1 John 2:1. How would you describe Jesus's role as an advocate?

Read Hebrews 7:25 (margin) and record your thoughts about the role Jesus plays.

Rather than condemn us, Jesus intercedes for us. He bridges the gap.

Therefore he is able, once and forever, to save those who come to God through him. He lives forever to intercede with God on their behalf.

(Hebrews 7:25)

Knowing that Jesus stands ready to serve as your Advocate, how can you walk more boldly in your faith?

We have a Savior, an Advocate, who not only pursues us but intercedes and speaks on our behalf. Allow that to sink in. Let it reassure you, friend. You are a daughter of the Creator of the universe. Chosen, pursued, and loved. That is your blessed assurance. Jesus is yours. And you belong to Him.

Prayer

- Thank God for His relentless love for you. Ask Him to show you someone who needs to also experience that kind of love from you.
- How can you share His love with someone in need today?

Video Viewer Guide
WEEK 4

Scriptures: John 3:16, 1 Peter 1:18-21, Ephesians 1:4-5, Zephaniah 3:17

Jesus's _____ _____ was never plan B. It was plan A all along.

God payed the _____ for your _____—a price that you could not afford to pay on your own.

Jesus's _____ for us was something God knew would be necessary from the beginning of _____.

God _____ in you.

Pursued in Our Unsavory Moments

NEW TESTAMENT ENCOUNTERS

Day 1

Settle

Take out a notepad and start a blessing list today. Thinking back to your earliest memories, write down the ways God has blessed you. If you can't finish it today, at least give it a good beginning and you can come back later to add to it. On your low days, pull out this list and read your blessings aloud as an act of thanks to your heavenly Father.

Focus

⁹*As Jesus was going on down the road, he saw a tax collector, Matthew, sitting at a tax collection booth. "Come and be my disciple," Jesus said to him, and Matthew jumped up and went along with him.*

¹⁰*Later, as Jesus and his disciples were eating dinner at Matthew's house, there were many notorious swindlers there as guests!*

¹¹*The Pharisees were indignant. "Why does your teacher associate with men like that?"*

¹²*"Because people who are well don't need a doctor! It's the sick people who do!" was Jesus' reply.* ¹³*Then he added, "Now go away and learn the meaning of this verse of Scripture,*

'It isn't your sacrifices and your gifts I want—I want you to be merciful.'

For I have come to urge sinners, not the self-righteous, back to God."

(Matthew 9:9-13 TLB)

Reflect

For years my local church has been involved with child sponsorship through Compassion International. But before we got involved, we did a lot of research because we didn't want to introduce our congregation to an organization that didn't do things well. So, we got to know some of their key leaders and asked hard questions about accountability and transparency. Honestly, we had a nagging concern that maybe the picture that hung on our refrigerator was a generic one. We wondered, *Is this child really out there and if so, how many sponsors does she really have?* So, we kept investigating. In fact, before pitching Compassion's sponsorship to our congregation we traveled with the organization to Africa to see behind the scenes how things are handled. The more we learned the more enthusiastic we became!

In our visit with them, we were most excited about meeting the child my family sponsored. Her name is Miremba. We had been told that we would be going to her village in Uganda, but would she really be there? When we arrived, children crowded around us but we didn't see her little face. We showed them Miremba's picture and asked if they knew her. Some of the children shouted her name and sprinted off. We waited, and about fifteen minutes later, a shy little girl cautiously came toward us. There she was! The child whose picture had hung in our kitchen for months was now standing before us.

As we learned her story, we discovered that her path has been one of pain. Her father had passed away, her mother had abandoned her, and she is now in the care of her father's second wife who has another eight children. Miremba's life is hard. Extreme poverty has taken a toll on her. It became our goal to help make this child feel special. We wanted her to know that she is loved by us and by God. We hugged her, gave her a few small gifts, told her she was precious, but honestly, during that first meeting she wouldn't even meet our eyes. I don't think she said a word to us. Her older cousin, Zahara, stayed by her side almost protectively and smiled and thanked us for loving Miremba. It was a sweet but sad encounter.

We stay in touch with Miremba regularly and have even returned a few times to visit her. On our second trip, she was much warmer but she still didn't talk with us. We continued to love on her and told her she is special and chosen. But the wounds of life are deep for this sweet girl, so she remained cautious and distant. It was again a sweet but sad visit.

Since that first visit, our church has become involved with Compassion International ministries and we now sponsor about one thousand children. A year ago when we held another sponsorship drive, my daughter grabbed me and said, "I've found another child you have to sponsor!" Honestly, we already sponsor quite a few kids and I wasn't sure we should take on one more. I didn't want to disappoint my daughter, Alyssa, but we were doing our part already. She said, "Mom, just wait, you'll see. You're going to want to do this, I promise!"

In a stack of hundreds and hundreds of children, Alyssa had seen the packet for Zahara, Miremba's protective cousin we had met four years earlier. She was now seventeen and in need of someone to sponsor her so that she could get in school and receive medical care. Of course, we sponsored her, too.

A few months later we went again to Uganda. This time, we went to the village to see several children, including Zahra. When she saw us at a distance, she broke into a huge smile. She remembered us too. Over the course of the next few days, she must have hugged us dozens of times and thanked us for remembering her and choosing her from among all of the children. Her gratitude was precious, but what really caught my attention was Merimba's response. For the first time she began to speak to us. As we ate together, she reached over and took my husband's hand and held it gently. This was huge! And then before we left she looked right into my eyes and said very quietly, "You chose us. You chose us both."

Yes! Yes! Yes! You are chosen!

Who makes you feel special?

What do they do to make you feel chosen and loved?

This week, we will focus on encounters in the New Testament where Jesus pursues with passion unlikely candidates for His attention. Unsavory, rough, sinful, despised, even cruel—all words that could describe

[Jesus's] love is relentless in wanting to reach you and allow you to thrive as the beautiful woman of God He created you to be.

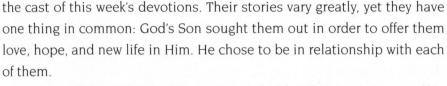

the cast of this week's devotions. Their stories vary greatly, yet they have one thing in common: God's Son sought them out in order to offer them love, hope, and new life in Him. He chose to be in relationship with each of them.

As we reflect on their stories, try to read with new eyes. Put yourself in their place and imagine what you would feel as Jesus approaches you in each unique encounter. My prayer is that these passages will come alive for you this week in ways you have never experienced. In many ways these stories are our stories. We are the unsavory, rough, sinful, despised—and perhaps even cruel at times. Yet Jesus pursues us! His love is relentless in wanting to reach you and allow you to thrive as the beautiful woman of God He created you to be.

In the beginning of Matthew 9, Jesus returns to His base of ministry, Capernaum. Situated at the north of the Sea of Galilee, it was a wealthy city, bustling with industry and culture. Because He spent a great deal of time in this area, He was probably well known and knew the people of the town. He would have known their reputations and occupations, including Matthew, the tax collector.

Tax collectors were an unpopular group. Roman authorities took bids for the right to collect taxes. A set amount was established to be paid to Rome, and the tax collector kept for himself anything above that amount. They became wealthy by collaborating with and preying on their own Jewish brothers and sisters. Being known for their harshness and lack of mercy in their financial collections made tax collectors despised by the people in their communities.

Matthew surely fit this description. Yet Jesus called him. What a shock that must have been to those in the crowd. Even the disciples must have murmured. But, surely the one most shocked must have been Matthew himself.

Read Matthew 9:9-13 (page 137) and reflect on the story by answering the following questions.

Who are the characters in this story?

How would you describe each of the characters?

Which of the characters are you most like? Why?

The teacher, the One who had just healed the paralyzed man, the One they said calmed the storms and healed leprosy was calling Matthew's name. This teacher, the healer, was choosing him, a tax collector. We can't know exactly what Matthew felt in that moment, but we do know this: he got up immediately and followed Jesus. In fact, in Luke's telling of this moment it says, "He left all, rose up, and followed Him" (Luke 5:28 NKJV).

I love the immediacy of Matthew's response. Jesus calls him and he responds. No questions, no excuses, no hesitation. He rose up, left all, and followed. Isn't that incredible?

I've often pondered what made Matthew so receptive to Jesus's invitation. So often when I feel Jesus calling to me, I hesitate. I want details. How will this work? Who will help? What will this cost me? But Matthew just got up and followed.

When have you been like Matthew, responding immediately to God's prompting?

When have you hesitated to respond faithfully?

Identify what causes you to hesitate so that you can be ready with a more trusting response to Christ in the future.

Matthew not only responds personally to Jesus but he also wants to give his friends the same opportunity. So, he holds a dinner party for scoundrels. Some translations call them tax collectors and sinners (NIV). The Message call them "crooks and riffraff." Sounds like a tough crowd. Matthew experienced the joy of being chosen and he wants to share that with those he knows. It doesn't seem to cross his mind that anyone would be too rough or rotten to sit at the table with Jesus. We'll talk more about this next week, but don't miss the point: once Matthew feels the love and pursuit of Jesus, he looks for ways to share that with those around him.

Friends, let's be like Matthew. When we feel the pursuit of God, we respond immediately!

Prayer

Listen to "Reckless Love" by Cory Asbury or another worship song of your choosing. As you listen, rest in the fact that you are chosen, pursued, and called to be God's child. Thank Him for that today and rest in His accepting and gracious Spirit.

Day 2

Settle

Close your eyes and listen for a few minutes. Fine-tune your senses to hear all that is around you—birds, traffic, the breeze, a cricket, kids playing. You may notice something that you were not aware of before. Ask God to give you ears to hear in new ways today—His voice, the needs of others, and the world around you.

Focus

18As Jesus was walking beside the Sea of Galilee, he saw two brothers, Simon called Peter and his brother Andrew. They were casting a net into the lake, for they were fishermen. 19"Come, follow me," Jesus said, "and I will send you out to fish for people." 20At once they left their nets and followed him.

21Going on from there, he saw two other brothers, James son of Zebedee and his brother John. They were in a boat with their father Zebedee, preparing their nets. Jesus called them, 22and immediately they left the boat and their father and followed him.

(Matthew 4:18-22 NIV)

Whoever says he abides in him ought to walk in the same way in which he walked.
(1 John 2:6 ESV)

Imitate God, therefore, in everything you do, because you are his dear children.
(Ephesians 5:1)

Reflect

As I mentioned earlier, I've been blessed to have several mentors in life and ministry. I've watched and studied these women and men and

tried to learn from them new skills, information, and habits in order to do my job well. But I have had a few mentors from whom I learned much more than new techniques and tools. I learned character, grace under fire, and what wisdom looks like with skin on. These are more than teachers; they are role models in my life. I have become something of a disciple to them, meaning I want to learn to be like them. Of course, my ultimate goal is to take on the character of Christ, but honestly, at times the easiest way for me to live that out is to learn from others who represent Him well.

Who could serve as a role model for you when it comes to the following categories? Write a name beside each one.

Anger

Disappointment

Success

Overcoming Failure

Disagreements

Making Decisions

Finances

Relationships

Spiritual Maturity

In Jesus's day, Jewish children (both boys and girls) at age five began to study Scripture under a rabbi in their local synagogue. As time progressed, there were milestones to reach, such as being able to recite and interpret the Torah. By the age twelve, the girls' education ended, and boys continued their religious studies but also learned a trade. A select group of promising students progressed with the hope that perhaps they would be called to become teachers also.

Rabbis would often travel from town to town quizzing the students in order to select the brightest to mentor. Once a disciple was selected, the rabbi would call to him "follow me." This was the indicator to everyone present that this student had been chosen to develop a special relationship with the teacher. This new disciple was then tasked to not only learn the teachings of his rabbi but also to take on his character and even live in his likeness.

If fact, an ancient Jewish blessing said, "May you be covered in the dust of your rabbi," meaning that students should follow their teacher so closely that as they traveled together, the disciple would be coated in the dust that the teacher kicked up from their sandals. It's a beautiful image showing how closely the disciple and teacher were to be connected.

Being singled out to become a disciple was a great honor afforded to only a few young men. The others went home to learn their families' trades. This was undoubtedly the case for Jesus's first disciples.

Read Matthew 4:18-22 (page 143).

Which four disciples are mentioned in these verses?

Peter and Andrew, along with James and John, did something when they heard Jesus call them. What did they do?

Peter, Andrew, James, and John had already been dismissed from their rabbinical studies to return home. They now spent their days fishing the Sea of Galilee. In essence, they had been passed over. They thought they had missed their shot. And then comes Jesus! When He calls to them, the Bible tells us clearly that they responded immediately.

As I have read these passages in the past, I've been puzzled as to how these fishing brothers could leave their jobs and family so quickly. But, as we learn the context of how disciples were called, the reason for their response becomes obvious. This was an opportunity they thought they'd never have. They had not been selected; by human standards they had not measured up. But then comes Jesus, who chooses them! The long-lost opportunity is offered. So, they immediately respond.

What dream seems to have passed you by?

Have you perhaps given up too soon? Are you ready to lay it before God again today and see what He has to say about it? Explain/respond.

When these four fishermen first began to follow Jesus they had lots of questions. They would often pull Jesus aside after He taught the crowds, wanting to know what He meant. What does this parable mean? How and when will this happen? Like all students, they had a great deal to learn. As they spent more time with Jesus, they matured and began to take on more and more Christlike qualities.

All disciples need time to become covered in the dust of their rabbi, but time will not create a solid coating of dust unless the disciple is following closely. True disciples follow at such a tight proximity that they learn more than facts, stories, and concepts. They begin to take on the manner and even character of the one they follow.

As we follow the progression of Peter, Andrew, James, and John, we see evidence of how they grow in maturity and in the fruits of the Spirit. Peter, for example, is quick with a sword to defend Jesus when He is arrested. However, after the Resurrection Peter lays down the sword and is quick to respond with the message of salvation instead of violence. As a result, instead of a soldier with a severed ear, we see thousands come to Christ through Peter's messages. He has grown to not only know the message of Jesus, but to embody His character. This is the goal of a mature disciple.

Read Philippians 2:1-11 below.

¹*Is there any encouragement from belonging to Christ? Any comfort from his love? Any fellowship together in the Spirit? Are your hearts tender and compassionate?* ²**Then make me truly happy by agreeing wholeheartedly with each other, loving one another, and working together with one mind and purpose.**

³**Don't be selfish; don't try to impress others. Be humble, thinking of others as better than yourselves.** ⁴**Don't look out only for your own interests, but take an interest in others, too.**

⁵**You must have the same attitude that Christ Jesus had.**

> ⁶**Though he was God,**
>   he did not think of equality with God
>   as something to cling to.
> ⁷**Instead, he gave up his divine privileges;**
>   he took the humble position of a slave
>   and was born as a human being.
> When he appeared in human form,
>   ⁸he humbled himself in obedience to God
>   and died a criminal's death on a cross.
>
> ⁹Therefore, God elevated him to the place of highest honor
>   and gave him the name above all other names,
> ¹⁰that at the name of Jesus every knee should bow,
>   in heaven and on earth and under the earth,
> ¹¹and every tongue declare that Jesus Christ is Lord,
>   to the glory of God the Father.

(Philippians 2:1-11)

What does this passage tell us about Jesus?

What instructions are we given? (v. 5)

When we place people on a pedestal, elevating them to a place of reverence, then we're in trouble. The One we are to imitate is Christ Himself.

In this world where we can follow people on social media, or follow someone's career path, or follow their rise to stardom, it's easy to confuse information with relationships. A disciple goes much deeper than surface-level imitation. A disciple becomes an imitator of the one he or she follows, trying to live into the values of the one he or she follows. Today, we actually see people devote themselves in a disciple-like fashion to those they follow on social media and in the entertainment world. Dressing like, acting like, and establishing values like others can become a form of reverence.

It's not necessarily wrong to learn from others who do things well. Think Joanna Gaines decor guidelines or Rachael Ray cooking tips. In fact, there is a lot of wisdom in learning from others. But when we place people on a pedestal, elevating them to a place of reverence, then we're in trouble. The One we are to imitate is Christ Himself. The One whose dust we want to be covered in is Jesus.

Reflect on 1 John 2:6. In what areas of life do you feel you are walking in the way in which Jesus did?

Read Ephesians 5:1. What would it look like for you to imitate God in the following areas?

At home:

At work:

With your family:

At church:

In a difficult relationship with:

Like the fishermen of Galilee, Jesus is calling to you today with the invitation to follow Him. It is not a casual invitation, however. It is the precious, privileged opportunity to enter into a personal relationship where you can walk closely with God's own Son. Don't miss the magnitude of being chosen for this honor. May you walk so closely that you, my friend, are covered in the dust of your Rabbi!

Prayer

Dear Jesus, thank You for inviting me to follow You. Today, I choose again to do just that. Help me to follow so closely that I am completely covered in Your dust. May I act and react as You would. Help me see people the way You do. Help me love them the way You do. Help me serve them the way You do. Amen.

Day 3

Settle

Before settling into your spot for your time with Jesus today, stand up and stretch. Really reach up high and out wide—breathe in deeply and allow your body to release tension so that you can come fresh before the Lord.

Focus

Jesus returned to the Mount of Olives, ²but early the next morning he was back again at the Temple. A crowd soon gathered, and he sat down and taught them. ³As he was speaking, the teachers of religious law and the Pharisees brought a woman who had been caught in the act of adultery. They put her in front of the crowd.

⁴"Teacher," they said to Jesus, "this woman was caught in the act of adultery. ⁵The law of Moses says to stone her. What do you say?"

⁶They were trying to trap him into saying something they could use against him, but Jesus stooped down and wrote in the dust with his finger. ⁷They kept demanding an answer, so he stood up again and said, "All right, but let the one who has never sinned throw the first stone!" ⁸Then he stooped down again and wrote in the dust.

⁹When the accusers heard this, they slipped away one by one, beginning with the oldest, until only Jesus was left in the middle of the crowd with the woman. ¹⁰Then Jesus stood up again and said to the woman, "Where are your accusers? Didn't even one of them condemn you?"

[11]"No, Lord," she said.

And Jesus said, "Neither do I. Go and sin no more."

(John 8:1-11)

This means that anyone who belongs to Christ has become a new person. The old life is gone; a new life has begun!

(2 Corinthians 5:17)

As far as the east is from the west,
     so far has he removed our transgressions from us.
          (Psalm 103:12 NIV)

Reflect

As I've shared before, early in my ministry I worked in the inner city. We never knew the challenges each day might bring. One especially memorable young woman who came through the doors was a prostitute. I'll call her Lyssa. Through a series of tragedies, her life had brought her to a rough place of struggling each day to survive. Lyssa and I were both in our early twenties, but our paths had been very different in reaching adulthood. She had come to the community center desperate for a better life, but she had no idea how to make that happen.

This occurred before we used phrases like "sex trafficking," but that was what was happening to her. She "belonged" to someone and had been told that if she didn't show up for "work," she would be hurt. At first I was at a loss. It was my first exposure to modern-day slavery. The details of her story that she honestly shared horrified me. This was in my hometown. The place where I took piano lessons and went to high school football games. How could this be?

As we began to formulate a plan for her escape and a new life, we realized that one of the obstacles she was facing was that she felt her life held no worth. She felt too damaged, too sinful, too far gone to believe there could be anything beautiful ahead for her.

The staff and I had worked on a safe house, clothing, an education path, and a temporary job situation for her so that she could leave her present life. But she couldn't embrace it. She simply did not feel worthy.

In working so furiously to formulate a plan for her, we had not taken the time to just love her. She needed safety, but she also just needed to be hugged and to hear that she was precious. Lyssa did not yet know that God loved her and that what had happened to her was not His plan; it was evil. Lyssa needed to feel pursued by God's amazing love. She needed to know that she could be washed clean and start her life anew in God's grace.

When have you needed a fresh start?

How have you felt God's cleansing in the past?

In what area of your life do you need cleansing today?

Second Corinthians 5:17 tells us that "anyone who belongs to Christ has become a new person. The old life is gone; a new life has begun!" This is the promise to all who come to know and trust Jesus with their lives. As we discover the love of Christ, it transforms us into new creations, revealing the character that God intended us to have from our birth. And Jesus proclaimed that this new life comes through Him (John 14:6).

Read John 8:1-11 (pages 150–151). Use your imagination to place yourself in the story. What do you see? What do you hear? What do you smell, taste, and touch? Use the space below to describe the scene.

What from this story sticks out the most to you? What seems to leap off the page?

When I read in John 8 about this woman who is infamously caught in the act of adultery, several questions come to mind. First, where is the guy? Why wasn't he thrown before Jesus, too? Second, what did Jesus write in the sand? Perhaps, he wrote the sins of those gathered in the crowd and then drew arrows at each person to signify He knew their dirty secrets too. Or perhaps, he wrote in the sand so the attention would shift from her (and her humiliated state) to Him, giving her a chance to gather her dignity and possibly some clothes. Third, after the crowd left and Jesus speaks to her, what did she do?

The Scriptures don't tell us any of these details. John doesn't give us the rest of her story, but I like to play it out in my head. Here's how it goes in my version: After the most humiliating and frightening moment of her life, after she has come face to face with stoning, she looks into the face of the One who says to her, "I don't condemn you. Go and sin no more." She is changed! From that moment on, she dedicates her life to serving Christ and to helping other young promiscuous women leave their sins behind and come to know the love of their Creator. She is not stuck in the humiliation or fear of that moment. She is not traumatized forever by the experience. She is healed in spite of it because of her encounter with Christ's love. What was meant to destroy her is the moment that brings her new life in Christ.

When have you faced a time that could have crushed you, but as you sought Jesus, you found new life in spite of the circumstance?

God yearns for us to find recovered and restored lives through Him.

Reflect on what you learned during that time.

The love and forgiveness of God is so deep and rich. Like Psalm 103:12 (page 151), Isaiah 1:18 beautifully reveals how God yearns for us to find recovered and restored lives through Him. "As far as east is from the west" and "as clean as freshly fallen snow"—the writers used these metaphors to help us understand that we are washed completely when we turn from sin and embrace God. Notice that Jesus says, "Go and sin no more" (John 8:11). He forgives her, but He also instructs her to leave this behavior behind. I like to imagine that this is exactly what she did.

But I don't know the end of her story, or of Lyssa's. In my optimism, I like to think they both went on to lead lives of tremendous ministry with other women trapped in similar circumstances. What I do know is that God loved them. He did not stand waiting to condemn them, but to offer them new life in Him. I know that no matter what they did, it was not enough to separate them from God if they chose to embrace Him.

In this week's devotional lessons, we have been looking at people who had life-altering encounters with Jesus. Through their experiences with Him they found forgiveness and purpose. Even at their lowest moments they found Jesus was pursuing them. And the same is true for you and me.

Prayer

As you pray today, confess before the Lord any area in your life that is not under His control. It may be language, an attitude, parenting, time management, or a habit. Offer that to Him, asking Him to forgive you for not being faithful and to help you live as a new creation in which His priorities become yours.

Day 4

Settle

Try something creative as you focus on God today. Draw Him a picture, sing Him a song, write Him a poem, or take a picture that expresses your love for Him and the beauty of His creation. Enjoy the effort of doing something new!

Focus

14"For if you forgive other people when they sin against you, your heavenly Father will also forgive you. 15But if you do not forgive others their sins, your Father will not forgive your sins.

(Matthew 6:14-15 NIV)

Your attitude should be the kind that was shown us by Jesus Christ.

(Philippians 2:5 TLB)

33Peter declared, "Even if everyone else deserts you, I will never desert you."

34Jesus replied, "I tell you the truth, Peter—this very night, before the rooster crows, you will deny three times that you even know me."

35"No!" Peter insisted. "Even if I have to die with you, I will never deny you!" And all the others disciples vowed the same.

(Matthew 26:33-35)

69Peter was sitting outside in the courtyard. A servant girl came over and said to him, "You were one of those with Jesus the Galilean."

⁷⁰But Peter denied it in front of everyone. "I don't know what you're talking about," he said.

⁷¹Later, out by the gate another servant girl noticed him and said to those standing around, "This man was with Jesus of Nazareth."

⁷²Again Peter denied it, this time with an oath. "I don't even know the man," he said.

⁷³A little later some of the other bystanders came over to Peter and said, "You must be one of them; we can tell by your Galilean accent."

⁷⁴Peter swore, "A curse on me if I'm lying—I don't know the man!" And immediately the rooster crowed.

⁷⁵Suddenly, Jesus' words flashed through Peter's mind: "Before the rooster crows, you will deny three times that you even know me." And he went away, weeping bitterly.

(Matthew 26:69-75)

"If you return to me, I will restore you
    so you can continue to serve me."
            (Jeremiah 15:19a)

Reflect

Okay, let's get honest for a moment. Whom have you not forgiven? Think about it. Perhaps you are a clean slate and absolutely no one comes to mind. At times I feel like that, but then something triggers a memory and there it is: the pain, the aggravation, maybe even anger is rekindled toward someone who hurt me, or worse, hurt someone close to me. I'm not proud of it, but sometimes it takes me a while to genuinely forgive someone who has hurt me deeply.

Eventually, though, I get there. In fact, I like to think I'm a great forgiver. But, before you give me credit for being super spiritual, you need to know that one of the primary reasons I forgive quickly is because I am moved by God's loving instruction to forgive as we have been forgiven. Scripture is really clear on the matter: "Be kind to one another, tender-hearted, forgiving each other, just as God in Christ also has forgiven you" (Ephesians 4:32 NASB), and "If you do not forgive others their sins, your Father will not forgive your sins" (Matthew 6:15 NIV). So, one of the reasons I am a good forgiver is because I'm aware of how desperately I need to be forgiven.

Whom have you struggled to forgive?

What feelings come to the surface when you think of them?

Whose forgiveness have you received in the past?

Which do you think more about—those you have forgiven or those who have forgiven you?

There's more to forgiveness than just wanting to be forgiven ourselves. As believers, we are to take on the likeness of Christ. Philippians 2:5 (TLB) says it this way: "Your attitude should be the kind that was shown us by Jesus Christ." Today we are going to look at His example and consider how best we can emulate it.

During His ministry, Jesus is loving toward everyone, but He is especially close to three of His disciples: Peter, James, and John. It's these three whom Jesus takes with Him on several occasions, such as the raising of Jairus's daughter (Mark 5:37), in the garden of Gethsemane (Mark 14:33), and at the Mount of Transfiguration (Matthew 17:1). These guys are more than ministry partners; they are close friends. Remember that as we look at a familiar passage.

Read Matthew 26:69-75 (pages 156–157). In the chart below, fill in the information about Peter's experience.

	Person Accusing	What They Said about Peter	Peter's Response
v. 69			
v. 71			
v. 73			

When we read of Peter's denial of Jesus on the night He is arrested, we can know that this was not a casual betrayal. Surely, Jesus felt a deep sense of hurt that Peter denied even knowing Him. Thank goodness that John and the women stayed close to Jesus throughout this long, lonely night.

When has someone reached out to you during a painful season?

Whom do you know struggling right now? How can you be present for them?

If ever there was a sin that we might consider unforgivable it would be to deny Jesus on the night of His greatest struggle. That seems like a biggie! But Jesus was not surprised by Peter's actions. In fact, He had already alerted Peter about it.

Read Matthew 26:33-35 (page 156).

What was Peter's pledge to Jesus?

What did Jesus predict about Peter?

How did Peter respond to Jesus?

"I tell you the truth, Peter—this very night, before the rooster crows, you will deny three times that you even know me" (Matthew 26:34). Jesus knew Peter would deny Him, but He also knew Peter would come back in hopes of forgiveness and restoration. In fact, before Peter denies Jesus, Jesus proclaims, "I have pleaded in prayer for you that your faith should not completely fail. So when you have repented and turned to me again, strengthen and build up the faith of your brothers" (Luke 22:32 TLB).

Read John 21:1-17. As you read, put yourself in the story as if you were Peter. What are you feeling during this interaction?

Take a look back at John 21:4-7 and consider what Jesus is feeling as He sees Peter jump from the boat and head to shore. Write your thoughts below.

Jesus knew that Peter's worst and best days lay ahead of him. His faith and ministry were stronger after his denial than it had ever been. As we see Peter preach and lead the church in the Book of Acts, he is no longer cowering or denying Jesus. Instead, he is proclaiming Christ crucified and resurrected boldly and publicly. Something has changed. When Jesus restores Peter during breakfast by the sea, He sends him off with a new sense of purpose, forgiven and clean.

What a shame it would have been if Peter had just wallowed in self-doubt and guilt for the rest of his life. What a missed opportunity that would have been. Jesus not only forgave Peter but He also restored and empowered him. When I put myself in Jesus's position, I wonder if I would have found it easier to talk with Thaddeus or Bartholomew at that little beachside brunch. I wouldn't have acted ugly, but I might have avoided Peter—the friend who wasn't there for me. But, Jesus pursues him instead.

Now, on the other hand, when I put myself in Peter's position, I don't wonder, I know I would have been tempted to direct my attention to Thad and Bart and avoid Jesus altogether. The shame would have been too great to bear. Instead of jumping from the boat toward Jesus, I might have been tempted to hide in the shadows. Just meeting Jesus's eyes would have been difficult. However, Peter had no reservations. He receives what Jesus is offering to him—forgiveness and a mission. Jesus tells Peter three times, "Feed my little sheep" (John 21:17). And that is exactly what Peter does. In the Book of Acts, for example, on the day of Pentecost Peter gives an impromptu impassioned sermon that leads to three thousand people accepting Jesus. This is not the same man who hid in the shadows. This man is responding to love offered to him by the One who pursued him.

Friend, Jesus pursues you too and wants to set you free from anything that is holding you back from your best life. I asked earlier who you need to forgive. It may be that the one in need of forgiveness today is you. If that is the case, then come before the Lord with anything about which you feel shame or guilt. Lay it before Him and allow this to be your moment of freedom as you receive His forgiveness once and for all.

Jesus pursues Peter in order to set him free of sin and to commission him for a powerful life of ministry. He wants to do the same for you. In

Jesus pursues you . . . and wants to set you free from anything that is holding you back from your best life.

these first five weeks of study we have focused on God's relentless pursuit of you, but in week 6 we will turn the focus a bit. As people who have received the relentless love of God, we are compelled to share that with others. Next week, we will put into action love that pursues others passionately and relentlessly.

Prayer

Receive what this Scripture offers you today, and offer praise to God for who He is and what He has done for you: "If you return to me, I will restore you so you can continue to serve me" (Jeremiah 15:19).

Day 5

Settle

What has troubled you this week? Write down your concerns on a sheet of paper and as an act of worship, lay them before the Lord. Close your eyes and allow God to take control of those troublesome issues. In the silence, trust Him to care for every need in your life. Allow His presence to soothe your soul.

Focus

Thomas, nicknamed the Twin, said to his fellow disciples, "Let's go, too—and die with Jesus."

(John 11:16)

[1]"Don't let your hearts be troubled. Trust in God, and trust also in me. [2]There is more than enough room in my Father's home. If this were not so, would I have told you that I am going to prepare a place for you? [3]When everything is ready, I will come and get you, so that you will always be with me where I am. [4]And you know the way to where I am going."

[5]"No, we don't know, Lord," Thomas said. "We have no idea where you are going, so how can we know the way?"

[6]Jesus told him, "I am the way, the truth, and the life. No one can come to the Father except through me. [7]If you had really known me, you would know who my Father is. From now on, you do know him and have seen him!"

(John 14:1-7)

²⁴*One of the twelve disciples, Thomas (nicknamed the Twin), was not with the others when Jesus came.* ²⁵*They told him, "We have seen the Lord!"*

But he replied, "I won't believe it unless I see the nail wounds in his hands, put my fingers into them, and place my hand into the wound in his side."

²⁶*Eight days later the disciples were together again, and this time Thomas was with them. The doors were locked; but suddenly, as before, Jesus was standing among them. "Peace be with you," he said.* ²⁷*Then he said to Thomas, "Put your finger here, and look at my hands. Put your hand into the wound in my side. Don't be faithless any longer. Believe!"*

²⁸*"My Lord and my God!" Thomas exclaimed.*

²⁹*Then Jesus told him, "You believe because you have seen me. Blessed are those who believe without seeing me."*

(John 20:24-29)

Reflect

Did you have a nickname growing up? In college I was often called JT, my maiden name being Twiggs. I'm not sure where it originated, but it was a fun, casual nickname. Lots of my buddies, especially the guys, called me that. It was a definite "friend zone" nickname. So, when I started dating this new guy named Jim Cowart and he called me JT, I didn't like it. Friend zone wasn't what I was hoping for with this one!

One day, early in our relationship, Jim walked up to me and said, "What's up, JT?" I remember looking up at him and saying, "I'd really like you to call me Jennifer." Something happened in that moment. It was like we both knew this relationship was destined for more than a friend zone nickname.

Sometimes we get nicknames that are fun, but others may be painful. Sally the Brave, Helen the True, Wise Evie. But what if your nickname immortalized one of your worst moments. That is what happens for one of Jesus's closest friends: Thomas.

Among the disciples there were several nicknames. James and John, for instance, were known as the Sons of Thunder (Mark 3:17). I wonder what their dad was like! Simon is often called the zealot, denoting most likely past political affiliations. The other Simon, whom Jesus renames Peter, which means "rock" or "stone" (Matthew 16:18). Now, that's a cool title! But what about the other James, not John's brother, but the one known as James the Lesser? That's a rough one. Thomas is referenced as the Twin several times. Then, of course, there is Judas the betrayer, but he earned that nickname.

John, through his writing, gives himself a nickname, "the disciple Jesus loved" (John 13:23), but does it count if you create the name yourself?

The one nickname that seems most undeserved is given to Thomas. Now it's not in the Bible this way, but it is probably the most well known of them all: "Doubting Thomas." Let's review his story. We don't know the specifics of how he was called to become a disciple, like we do with the fisherman brothers and Matthew. His name is simply listed among the disciples as we read in the Gospels. His highlight reel, as recorded in Scripture, comes down to a few important encounters. The first we read about is in John 11.

Read John 11:1-16.

Who was sick?

What did Jesus want to do?

Why did the disciples want to stay away from Judea? (v. 8)

What was Thomas's response to Jesus's desire to go to Judea? (v. 16)

Upon hearing that His dear friend Lazarus is sick, Jesus tells the disciples that He is headed back to Judea. During their last visit to the

14:1 *"Don't let your hearts be troubled. Trust in God, and trust also in me. 2 There is more than enough room in my Father's home. If this were not so, would I have told you that I am going to prepare a place for you? 3 When everything is ready, I will come and get you, so that you will always be with me where I am. 4 And you know the way to where I am going."*

5 *"No, we don't know, Lord," Thomas said. "We have no idea where you are going, so how can we know the way?"* 6 *Jesus told him, "I am the way, the truth, and the life. No one can come to the Father except through me. 7 If you had really known me, you would know who my Father is. From now on, you do know him and have seen him!"*

(John 14:1-7)

Jerusalem region, some of the Jews had tried to stone Jesus, so the disciples discouraged Jesus from returning there. But Thomas bravely speaks up in John 11:16 and says, "Let's go, too—and die with Jesus." Thomas knows that heading back into Judea may be a death sentence for them all, but he is ready to go when Jesus commands. Based on this interaction alone, Thomas the Brave seems like a more appropriate nickname.

When have you faced real danger for following Jesus? When have you suffered for your faith? How did you handle it?

Read John 14:1-7 (in the margin), another famous interaction between Thomas and Jesus. Based on this account, what nickname could Thomas have received?

What is a nickname you've been called?

What is a nickname would you want Jesus to give you? Why?

I'd love to hear your nickname answers. By the way, Jim has called me a lot of other nicknames over the years: Jen, Jenny, Honey, but JT has never been one of them. We moved past the JT friend zone, thank goodness!

The third interaction where Thomas is singled out by name takes place after the Resurrection.

Read John 20:24-29 (page 164). Which disciple missed out on one of Jesus's appearances after the Resurrection?

What did this disciple say to the others?

Why do you think he refused to believe his friends?

Whom does Jesus single out when He appears to the disciples eight days later?

How do you think Thomas might have felt?

In John 20:19, Jesus appears to the disciples for the first time after His resurrection. They are gathered behind locked doors, but Scripture tells us that suddenly He was standing among them. And then before He leaves them, verse 22 says that He breathed on them and said, "Receive the Holy Spirit." This is a powerful moment. Imagine their relief, joy, and amazement! But Thomas was not there.

Maybe he had a cold, maybe he ran out to buy bread, maybe he was grieving alone after the Crucifixion. We don't know why he wasn't present when Jesus first appears to His disciples. But his fellow disciples told him, "We have seen the Lord!" Thomas replied, "I won't believe it unless I see the nail wounds in His hands, put my fingers into them, and place my hand into the wound in His side."

From this statement comes the famous moniker "Doubting Thomas." But let's challenge the label for a moment. Was he doubting, or did he just want to investigate in order to know the truth for himself? After all, hearing that someone you saw buried just appeared miraculously inside a locked room is a lot to process.

"If you look for me wholeheartedly, you will find me."

(Jeremiah 29:13)

"Keep on asking, and you will receive what you ask for. Keep on seeking, and you will find. Keep on knocking, and the door will be opened to you."

(Matthew 7:7)

Eight days after Thomas expresses his desire to see Jesus for himself, he gets the opportunity. Jesus appears to him. I don't read Jesus's tone as a harsh one. In fact, it's precious. Jesus basically says to him, "Hey, I heard you. Here, touch my wounds and let all of your doubts and fears be erased. I'm really here. It's okay to believe! At once Thomas cried out, "My Lord and my God!" (John 20:28).

Jesus can handle our questions. In fact, as we seek Him, we find that He meets us in our search. This is not a game of hide-and-go-seek where the hider doesn't want to be found. When we search for Jesus and when we come to Him with our questions, we actually find that He was already pursuing us.

Read Jeremiah 29:13 and Matthew 7:7 (in the margin).

What do these verses teach us about God's attitude toward us?

Circle the verbs in these verses. What do they tell us to do if we want to experience Christ?

Thomas had doubts and questions. What questions do you have for God?

What doubts have you had? How have those doubts affected your faith journey?

As far as we know, the label "Doubting Thomas" wasn't used during his lifetime. But, if it had been it would have been a misnomer. What's more appropriate is "Thomas the Brave Seeker." In fact, when I get to heaven and run into Thomas, I think I'll skip the nickname of "doubting" and go straight to "brave."

Perhaps you, like Thomas, have been labeled by a moment that doesn't represent your true heart. Or perhaps you have doubts that hold you back in your faith. Today you can lay them before the Lord.

At the end of Thomas's interaction with Jesus in John 20, did you notice that you are mentioned? You are! Look again. Jesus says, "You believe because you have seen me. Blessed are those who believe without seeing me" (John 20:29). You and I are "those" people Jesus was talking about here—the ones who believe without physically encountering Jesus. And we are blessed as we do what Thomas did. Voice your doubts and ask your questions. God will meet you there. He will pursue you as you seek Him.

Voice your doubts and ask your questions. God will meet you there.

Prayer

As you pray today, reveal to God any labels you carry that you want to shed. Ask Him to give you a nickname, something unique to your relationship with Him, and sit quietly for a moment and listen for Him to respond.

Insert your name here as you pray this Scripture as a declaration and means of thanksgiving back to God today:

Even before he made the world, God loved _____

and chose _____ *in Christ to be holy and without*

fault in his eyes (Ephesians 1:4). Thank You, Lord, for choosing me!

Video Viewer Guide
WEEK 5

Scriptures: Luke 23:32-43, Philippians 2:14, Psalm 56:3, Acts 16:31,
John 3:16, 2 Peter 3:9

The path to heaven is amazingly _____.

No matter what you've done, God is _____ to you.

There are no right _____ necessary to receive salvation.

Week 6

Pursued for the Sake of Others

PARTICIPATING IN GOD'S RESCUE MISSION

Day 1

Settle

Find your favorite spot at home and get comfortable. Maybe it's on a porch, snuggled up with a pet, or in a big comfy chair. Take a few deep breaths and allow the silence of being in God's presence to soothe your soul and bring you peace.

Focus

⁹If you openly declare that Jesus is Lord and believe in your heart that God raised him from the dead, you will be saved. ¹⁰For it is by believing in your heart that you are made right with God, and it is by openly declaring your faith that you are saved. ¹¹As the Scriptures tell us, "Anyone who trusts in him will never be disgraced." ¹²Jew and Gentile are the same in this respect. They have the same Lord, who gives generously to all who call on him. ¹³For "Everyone who calls on the name of the LORD will be saved."

¹⁴But how can they call on him to save them unless they believe in him? And how can they believe in him if they have never heard about him? And how can they hear about him unless someone tells them?

(Romans 10:9-14)

¹⁹Go and make disciples of all nations, baptizing them in the name of the Father and of the Son and of the Holy Spirit, ²⁰and teaching them to obey everything I have commanded you. And surely I am with you always, to the very end of the age.

(Matthew 28:19-20 NIV)

Reflect

I began writing this study during the COVID-19 crisis. As I write this, there is not yet a vaccine or cure. If someone were to develop a vaccine or cure and not offer it, that would be

criminal. The loving, humanitarian, compassionate thing to do would be to freely offer the solution in order for others to find healing. The same is true for cancer, Alzheimer's, AIDS, and every other disease ravaging people around the world. If and when cures are found, they must be shared.

Those of us who follow Jesus have something even more precious than a COVID cure. In a manner of speaking, we have the antidote to sin, the prescription for peace, and the remedy for eternal death. As people of God, we receive this cure when we accept Jesus as our Savior and repent of our sins—a cure that is essentially a loving relationship established on God's grace. From that point on, we enjoy God's presence and purpose, but we are also commanded to share this antidote—this good news—with those who have yet to receive it.

Let's think about the mission of Christ again. Luke 19:10 sums it up so well: "The Son of Man came to seek and to save the lost." God sent His Son on a mission to rescue all who are willing to repent of their sins and accept Him as Lord of their life. Jesus goes to great lengths to show us how deeply God loves all people. In Luke 15, we see the famous three parables of the lost sheep, coin, and boys. The point of each of these stories is that God is passionate about restoring that which is lost.

As His followers, Jesus commissions us to share that passion. As His children, we are to take on the family business of loving people and sharing the message of Christ with everyone everywhere. While on earth, Jesus leaves us with clear instructions. We, His disciples, are to continue the rescue mission. This passage is famously referred to as the Great Commission.

Read Matthew 28:19-20 (page 173).

Rewrite the verses—also known as the Great Commission—in your own words here:

Who followed the Great Commission by telling you about Jesus?

Have you ever told someone else about Jesus's love and forgiveness? If so, what was that experience like?

So far in this study, we have focused on God's relentless pursuit of you. You are loved, you are chosen, and you will be pursued by your heavenly Father every day of your life. That will never change. But, this week we are going to shift our focus and look at how we can share what we have received. We will explore how we can model what has been done for us. As those who have been pursued and found, we now have the privilege and responsibility to share that same love with others.

Do a quick faith-sharing self-assessment by circling the appropriate number. (1 being never, 5 being all the time)

How often do you:

invite someone to church with you?

1   2   3   4   5

invite someone to your Bible study?

1   2   3   4   5

share your faith story one-on-one?

1   2   3   4   5

share your faith publicly?

1   2   3   4   5

develop friendships with nonbelievers?

1   2   3   4   5

pray for those living far from God?

1   2   3   4   5

God is passionate about pursuing all people and asks you to become part of that pursuit.

Becoming intentional in sharing our faith is actually an act of obedience. Jesus doesn't suggest we do this; He commands it.

Based on what you've learned about God's pursuit of you, why do you think Jesus commands His followers to make disciples?

What questions, fears, doubts, or hesitations do you have about telling someone else about God's love for her or him?

God is passionate about pursuing all people and asks you to become part of that pursuit. Figuring out how to do that can be tricky. We don't want to be so aggressive that we alienate people. And we don't want to be so passionate that we come off as kooks. Because we don't want to offend anyone, embarrass ourselves, and sometimes, because we just don't know quite what to do, we often do nothing. But we can and must tell others about Jesus in real and life-changing ways.

For several years I led an accountability group of high school girls. They created a seven-point covenant that we agreed we would try to live into every week. Every Tuesday morning at 7 a.m. we met to encourage one another and hold one another accountable. Among the items on the list of things we challenged one another to were performing a random act of kindness weekly, spending time in prayer and Bible study daily, sharing our faith at least weekly, and inviting someone to church weekly. The random act of kindness and personal quiet time were easy commitments for me to keep. But having those teenage girls hold me accountable for inviting someone to church and sharing my faith weekly stretched my evangelistic skill set.

In wanting to set a good example for them, I got serious about upholding this covenant. I prayed that God would open my eyes to opportunities and, almost miraculously, there they were. At the grocery store, pumping gas, at the gym, I found myself looking for opportunities to share my faith. The opportunity to invite people to church presented itself everywhere—when I was looking for it. I became passionate about getting to know people far from God. I wanted to know their stories. I wanted to develop real friendships and I wanted to earn the privilege of sharing Jesus with them. Honestly, until that point, I would have told you that I had always been passionate about Christ. But, what began to change was my conviction to pursue others in order that they would know Him, too. I began to share Jesus's passion to pursue the people who needed to hear about God's love.

Read Romans 10:9-14 (page 173).

According to Paul, how can a person be saved? (vv. 9-10)

Who has the opportunity to do this? (vv. 11-13)

What dilemma does Paul present? (v. 14)

Becoming a follower of Jesus means believing in who Jesus is and what He has done for you. Nobody is excluded from that invitation. Everyone is welcome at the table of His grace. However, people can't become a follower of Jesus if they don't hear about Him. And they can't hear about Him unless somebody tells them.

You are the someone in this passage, my friend. And so am I. How will others receive the gift of grace if we do not share it with them? The life-saving cure to eternal death is found through Jesus. To not intentionally and freely share that with everyone possible is like withholding the vaccine for a virus or disease. It's wrong. So, here's the question we will delve into this week: how do we share Christ with a world so desperately in need of His love and salvation?

I invite you to join me in making a commitment to God to join Him in His pursuit of those who don't yet know Him. Make it part of your life's mission to be intentional in sharing Christ.

Prayer

As you pray today, ask God to unleash within you a new passion for those who do not yet know Him. Ask Him for wisdom and a winsome manner in which to love others in ways that lead them to the cross.

Day 2

Settle

Today, start your time with the Lord creatively! If you play an instrument, begin by playing it for the Lord. If you're artistic, draw as an act of worship. If neither of those appeal to you, then just put pen to paper and list the beautiful things of God's creation for which you are grateful.

Focus

But in your hearts revere Christ as Lord. Always be prepared to give an answer to everyone who asks you to give the reason for the hope that you have. But do this with gentleness and respect.

(1 Peter 3:15 NIV)

45Philip found Nathanael and told him, "We have found the one Moses wrote about in the Law, and about whom the prophets also wrote—Jesus of Nazareth, the son of Joseph."

46"Nazareth! Can anything good come from there?" Nathanael asked.

"Come and see," said Philip.

(John 1:45-46 NIV)

I pray that your partnership with us in the faith may be effective in deepening your understanding of every good thing we share for the sake of Christ.

(Philemon 1:6 NIV)

Reflect

"Who is your One?"

Jim and I were asked this question recently while doing some leadership training. Our ministry coach looked at us and asked, "Who is your One?'" Immediately, we both said, "Jesus." God, Jesus, or the Bible is usually the right church response when you're not sure of the answer, right? But he said, "Nope, try again. Who is your One?" We pointed at each other. As spouses, we thought, maybe that's what he meant. So I said, "Jim is my One." Wrong again. Now honestly, we were frustrated. What was he wanting? So we asked him to narrow it down for us.

He said, "What I want to know is, who is the One person in your life for whom your heart is breaking because he or she is living far from God? Who is that One person you are praying for and believing in faith for, that they may come to know and love Jesus?"

Oh, that One. Hmmm, no one specifically came to my mind.

After many years in ministry, I didn't have an immediate response. I mean, I know some people who don't know Jesus personally, but to say that my heart aches for them daily and that I am pursuing them through prayer and invitation would not have been truthful.

Now, my husband and I are church planters. Evangelism is at the core of who we are and how we do ministry. Since beginning the church in 2001, we have seen more than four thousand people accept Jesus as their Savior. It's been an incredible journey and we have really tried to create a culture that welcomes people far from God. But (I hate that there is a but here) after being asked that question, we realized we were not as intentional as we had once been about reaching those far from God. We didn't mean to drift, but we did. Without realizing it, we had become so occupied with the care and discipleship of those inside the church that we had begun to neglect the work of reaching out to those in our community who had not yet found God relevant in their lives. It took an intentional effort to shift our focus back to reaching people far from God. Unless we're intentional, we all tend to drift.

So, let me ask you: Who is your One?

Have you drifted from the Great Commission—the command to make disciples in Matthew 28:19-20? If so, how do you think that drift began?

How have you reached out to your One in the past?

Has it been effective? If not, what barriers have you faced?

Make a list here of those in your family or friend group who do not know Jesus personally.

If that list is short, where might you look to make genuine friendships with people living far from God? (social groups, the gym, clubs, etc.)

I've known Jesus since I was a teenager. My vocation is full-time ministry. So, most of the people I know and hang out with are seriously committed to Christ. And that's great! But, it doesn't give me a deep pool for sharing my faith on a regular basis. So, in order to live out the Great Commission on a personal level, I've had to get creative.

For instance, as we are living in this socially distanced environment with the virus, I've been burdened with how to love on people struggling through this pandemic without God. Surely, people have spiritual questions about what's happening in our world. Surely, they are hurting and need to know that this world is not the end. So, just yesterday, I reached out to one of my friends who is still pretty new to the Christian faith and asked her if she thought her friends who were not believers would be interested in a Zoom group where they could ask their God questions and have someone pray for them. She called me back in an hour and said, "How many people do you want in this group? I'm already at thirty!"

She was surprised at how quickly they said yes, but I wasn't surprised at all. First, when people are hurting, they are more open to things that bring hope and healing. And second, I know my friend. When she loves people, she loves them hard. So, when the invitation came from her, someone they trusted, they said yes based on the love she had shown them in the past. All we had to do was open a door. (Now we just have to hope I don't botch it up from here!)

So often, people are ready to hear truth and explore faith when it's offered with gentleness and respect.

Read 1 Peter 3:15.

What important truth about sharing your faith is mentioned in this verse?

What do you think it means to show gentleness and respect to a person?

If you had the opportunity, how would you share Christ in less than three minutes? Take the time to write out a short version of your faith story. Remember, attention spans are short and rarely do people give us time to hear the full story.

Since being asked about our One, Jim and I have become even more committed to living into the Great Commission. But, honestly, as long-time followers of Christ it takes effort. We've become intentionally focused on seizing and even creating opportunities to develop relationships with people far from God. Over time our goal is to love them well enough to earn the privilege of sharing Jesus with them.

If you have been a Christian for a long time, you may also find yourself primarily surrounded by other followers of Christ. If so, you may need to get creative in creating opportunities to rub shoulders with people who don't know Jesus.

But, maybe that is not your story. Maybe your circles are such that you have tons of opportunities to interact with people living far from God. If so, great! Get prepared. What will your strategy be? How can you share your faith gently and respectfully, like Peter instructs us to? If that seems overwhelming, then just take your cues from Nathanael, one of the disciples.

We who have come to know the love of Jesus need to help others find it, too.

Read John 1:45-46.

What was Nathanael's approach for telling people about Jesus?

How did he respond to opposition?

When Nathanael enthusiastically tells his friend Philip about meeting Jesus, he gets a less than enthusiastic response. But Nathanael is not deterred. Instead, he just offers an invitation: "come and see." If you don't feel well equipped to share your faith or tell your story, then at least invite people to come and see for themselves.

A popular saying in churches today is "Found people find people." Another way of saying that could be "Pursued people pursue people." Both phrases encourage the same goal: We who have come to know the love of Jesus need to help others find it, too.

Pray

As you pray today, ask the Lord to:

- give you a heart to share Him with others,
- open your eyes to the opportunities around you to meet lost people and share God's love for them, and
- identify the One in your life.

Day 3

Settle

Tune out the distractions of life today by listening to a favorite song. Allow the words and melody to bring peace to you.

Focus

¹Now Jesus learned that the Pharisees had heard that he was gaining and baptizing more disciples than John—²although in fact it was not Jesus who baptized, but his disciples. ³So he left Judea and went back once more to Galilee.

⁴Now he had to go through Samaria. ⁵So he came to a town in Samaria called Sychar, near the plot of ground Jacob had given to his son Joseph. ⁶Jacob's well was there, and Jesus, tired as he was from the journey, sat down by the well. It was about noon.

⁷When a Samaritan woman came to draw water, Jesus said to her, "Will you give me a drink?" ⁸(His disciples had gone into the town to buy food.)

⁹The Samaritan woman said to him, "You are a Jew and I am a Samaritan woman. How can you ask me for a drink?" (For Jews do not associate with Samaritans.)

¹⁰Jesus answered her, "If you knew the gift of God and who it is that asks you for a drink, you would have asked him and he would have given you living water."

¹¹"Sir," the woman said, "you have nothing to draw with and the well is deep. Where can you get this living water? ¹²Are you greater than our father Jacob, who gave us the well and drank from it himself, as did also his sons and his livestock?"

¹³Jesus answered, "Everyone who drinks this water will be thirsty again, ¹⁴but whoever drinks the water I give them will never thirst. Indeed, the water I give them will become in them a spring of water welling up to eternal life."

¹⁵The woman said to him, "Sir, give me this water so that I won't get thirsty and have to keep coming here to draw water."

¹⁶He told her, "Go call your husband and come back."

¹⁷"I have no husband," she replied.

Jesus said to her, "You are right when you say you have no husband. ¹⁸The fact is, you have had five husbands, and the man you now have is not your husband. What you have said is quite true."

(John 4:1-18 NIV)

(You can read this entire interaction in John 4.)

Many of the Samaritans from that town believed in him because of the woman's testimony.

(John 4:39 NIV)

Let the redeemed of the LORD say so.
(Psalm 107:2a ESV)

Reflect

Recently I had the opportunity to spend the afternoon with a six-year-old. Her parents were tied up, and I volunteered to hang out with her a while and then take her to her first-ever piano lesson. For a mom of young-adult kids, it was a fun afternoon for me. She was a little nervous at the idea of her first lesson, so I thought it would be helpful to distract her. We made cookies first, and then on the way to the lesson, I began asking her questions to keep her mind busy. After breaking the ice with light conversation, she took the lead and said, "Now Mrs. Jen, let's talk about heaven." Sounded great to me. So, I asked, "What do you think heaven is like?" Quickly, she responded, "Well first, you know, of course, in heaven Bibles are made out of rainbows." Hmm. Nope, I didn't know that. Interesting. She shared other creative thoughts and then I asked, "Since heaven is so awesome, why do you think God leaves us here on earth? What do you think He wants us to do?"

I glanced in the rearview mirror at this little cutie as her face intensified and then she said, "Miss Jen, you know this! We are here to help get people to heaven, so they can join us where we are already going."

Wow. This little lady gets it. Our primary goal as believers is to love God and love others in real and practical ways, ways that point them to Jesus. It doesn't get much more practical than helping people find the love and eternal security found in Christ.

As you imagine heaven, with whom do you look forward to reuniting?

Whom are you concerned may not be heaven-bound at this point in their lives?

As we travel through the stories of Jesus, we see that He often goes out of His way to connect with people far from God. For example, one of my favorite interactions recorded in the Bible is of the woman of Samaria whom Jesus meets at Jacob's well.

Read John 4:1-18 (pages 185–186).

Who are the two characters in this story?

What important fact is found in verse 4?

> Our primary goal as believers is to love God and love others in real and practical ways, ways that point them to Jesus.

What was so unusual about this encounter?

How did Jesus turn the conversation toward religious things?

There are so many nuances to this story that make it intriguing to me. First, Scripture says, "He had to go through Samaria" on his way from Judea to Galilee (v. 4). Samaria would not have been the direct route as He traveled from the south up to the northern Galilee region. Perhaps this is an indication that He had to go through Samaria in order to pursue this woman and the Samaritan village that she would then impact.

Second, Jesus meets this woman at an unlikely time. It's noon, the hottest part of the day, in one of the hottest areas on earth. This would not be a time when He would likely come upon a woman drawing water. But this woman, because of her broken past and soiled reputation, doesn't go early in the morning to draw water like the other women of the community. She avoids the crowd so she can also avoid the gossip, glares, and snide remarks she would most likely receive.

Another noteworthy element of this interaction is that Jesus addresses her directly. Obviously, she is shocked that a Jewish man breaks custom and speaks not only to a woman, but to a Samaritan woman.

> [7]Jesus said to her, "Will you give me a drink?" [8](His disciples had gone into the town to buy food.)
>
> [9]The Samaritan woman said to him, "You are a Jew and I am a Samaritan woman. How can you ask me for a drink?" (For Jews do not associate with Samaritans.)
> (John 4:7-9 NIV)

Jesus speaks directly to her and it quickly becomes apparent that He knows exactly who she is. He is not shocked by her past. He doesn't shun her, but he does confront her with the truth while offering her the hope of knowing Him personally.

It's also interesting that upon meeting Jesus, this woman leaves her water jar and goes back into town to talk to the very people who shun her and share the good news of meeting the Messiah. The weight of her sins seems to be lifted, or at least outweighed, by the joy of sharing about the One she has just met personally.

> *Then, leaving her water jar, the woman went back to the town and said to the people, "Come, see . . ."*
>
> (John 4:28 NIV)

But, perhaps, the most impactful part of this encounter is that her life change leads to the life change of many others. She who had been pursued immediately pursued others.

> *Many of the Samaritans from that town believed in him because of the woman's testimony.*
>
> (John 4:39 NIV)

Jesus waits for her. He knows her. His plan includes her. And in response to that loving pursuit, she shares His message with those around her. Psalm 107:2 says, "Let the redeemed of the Lord say so." She is saying so!

I've had the opportunity to visit this well twice. It is a holy place for me. I imagine Jesus meeting me there. As special as it is, there are some uncomfortable moments as I picture Him confronting me with the sin in my life like He did the woman of Samaria. But the overriding emotion is intimate and precious. That God's Son is invested personally in each of our stories is incredible. That He knows us, pursues us, and loves us is overwhelming. But, in the next phase of the story, we have the opportunity to move into action. As I left the well each time, I have felt a recommissioning to be like the woman at the well. I too want to go and share about the One whom I have met. Hopefully my story (and yours) will end like hers, and many others will believe because we played a small role in pointing them to Jesus.

Prayer

- Spend the bulk of your prayer time today lifting up those you know who do not yet have a relationship with Jesus.
- Thank God for pursuing you and ask Him to give you a passion to do the same for others.
- Invite God to interrupt you today in order to share His love and His message with someone who needs to be pursued.

Day 4

Settle

Sing, hum, or listen to the words of the classic hymn "Amazing Grace." Let the words linger: "Amazing Grace! How sweet the sound that saved a wretch like me! I once was lost, but now am found; was blind, but now I see."

Focus

⁵*Walk in wisdom toward outsiders, making the best use of the time.* ⁶*Let your speech always be gracious, seasoned with salt, so that you may know how you ought to answer each person.*

(Colossians 4:5-6 ESV)

⁹*Don't just pretend to love others. Really love them. Hate what is wrong. Hold tightly to what is good.* ¹⁰*Love each other with genuine affection, and take delight in honoring each other.* ¹¹*Never be lazy, but work hard and serve the Lord enthusiastically.*

(Romans 12:9-11)

And I pray that the sharing of your faith may become effective for the full knowledge of every good thing that is in us for the sake of Christ.

(Philemon 1:6 ESV)

Reflect

My son, Josh, returned from a wedding reception recently, where he had been seated with other college-aged students from various faith backgrounds. Friends professing belief in Hinduism, atheism, Islam, and Christianity were gathered together in a really friendly setting. Out of curiosity he said, "Okay, I want to ask you guys something. And I want to be respectful as I do, so help me out if I don't ask this well: during the prayers today during the ceremony, what were you thinking?"

Their responses were kind. Several said they bowed their heads out of respect. One young man said, "I tried to feel the emotion of what the prayer was trying to convey." It was a good-natured exchange. Then Josh said, "So, here's my dilemma, guys. Put yourself in my shoes. I truly believe that the only way to heaven is through Jesus. And I care about you. I don't want to offend you or alienate you. But if I really believe that Jesus is the only way to heaven, and if I really love you, then I am absolutely compelled to look for ways to share my faith with you. Anything else would be like me not caring about your eternity." He wasn't sure how that would be received, but the young Muslim man looked at him and said, "I respect that actually and I appreciate it."

That was several weeks ago. But just today Josh said to me again, "Remember those guys at the wedding? I really care about them. I'm playing the long game here, because I really don't want them to miss heaven. I can't stand the thought that they wouldn't be there."

As I've processed this whole interaction, I have realized that there were several components that helped the encounter go well, as well as things I can learn. First, a casual friendship already existed between the people involved. Relationships matter. Without a solid basis of friendship, people may feel like they are our Christian project and no one wants to feel like that! Second, Josh took the time to listen to them and really hear their points of view. Third, the whole conversation was bathed in respect and sincerity. And last, there was no secret agenda. Josh was clear in stating that he loved them and wanted them to know the same Jesus that he knew.

As people who have been pursued we are compelled to pursue others!

Who does your heart break for?

How can you begin to pray for them?

Read Colossians 4:5-6 and Romans 12:9-11 again (page 191), and think about how you can best live out these passages. Write your thoughts below:

Colossians 4:5-6:

Romans 12:9-11:

God was so consumed with passion for us that He sent Jesus to earth to pursue us. In return He wants us to pursue others. I am one of the redeemed. If you are too, then it's our responsibility to share Jesus with those around us. But we often run into a problem when it comes to sharing our faith. Sometimes, our passion for the lost turns cold.

Let me give you an example. Several years ago, our church noticed an interesting trend. As we greeted and reached out to our first-time attenders, we realized that most of them had been invited by their friends who attended but were not yet believers. In other words, most of our visitors were coming as the guests of people who weren't yet sure what they themselves believed. This was really interesting! Our pre-believing crowd were our best inviters.

The other notable inviters in our crowd included new believers and children. Do you see who is missing from the list? The mature believers! People like me and perhaps like you!

This was such an important finding that we began to do some research. We found that those newest to the message and hope of Christ were most excited about sharing with others what they had found. They were experiencing life change and their enthusiasm was contagious. Many of

them had come in the door with addictions, troubled marriages, broken spirits, and emotional baggage. Through Jesus, they were finding hope and life change and they wanted to share what they had found.

Yet, for many who had been believers for years, possibly even decades, their passion to share their faith was not at the top of their priorities. Could it be that, without meaning to, they had drifted from their first love? Can we really be faithful Christ followers if we are not sharing Christ with others?

In Revelation, Jesus gives an accounting to the churches of how well they have lived out their faith. It's almost a spiritual report card. Some have done really well, like Philadelphia and Smyrna. Some are struggling, like the church at Ephesus, which receives this report:

> [3]"You have persevered and have patience, and have labored for My name's sake and have not become weary. [4]Nevertheless I have this against you, that you have left your first love."
>
> (Revelation 2:3-4 NKJV)

Still some of the other churches receive a strong reprimand. To the church in Sardis, for example, we read, "You have a reputation for being alive—but you are dead" (Revelation 3:1). Then, perhaps, the harshest warning is given to Laodicea.

Read Revelation 3:15-16 in the margin.

How is the church described?

Why would being cold toward the things of God be better than being lukewarm?

"I know your deeds, that you are neither cold nor hot. I wish you were either one or the other! So, because you are lukewarm—neither hot nor cold—I am about to spit you out of my mouth."

(Revelation 3:15-16 NIV)

When I think of lukewarm I often think about milk. Cold milk is great—especially with a yummy chocolate dessert. Hot milk is also great—on a cold winter day. But lukewarm milk—yuck. Apparently, God feels very strongly about believers who lack passion in living out their faith.

What type of report would your church receive today?

What type of report would you receive personally?

The more we receive what God has done for us, the more likely we are to share it with those so desperately in need of Him.

Dear friend, my prayer for you is that you would become consumed with a passion to love others deeply. As we learn to rest in knowing that we are loved and pursued by our heavenly Father, it frees us to offer that love in great big doses to those around us. We can take our eyes off of ourselves and focus on the needs of others. The more we receive what God has done for us, the more likely we are to share it with those so desperately in need of Him.

Prayer

Take the time to read back through the Scriptures in our Focus section today. Allow those words to guide you as you communicate with God today.

Father, like Paul prayed for Philemon, I pray that the sharing of my faith would be effective in every good thing! Help me, Lord. Amen.

Day 5

Settle

Take a deep breath and slowly exhale. Do this several times. And as you breathe in, invite the Holy Spirit to fill you. As you exhale, release the stress and distractions that would keep you from enjoying this time with your heavenly Father. Today you may want to listen to "Friend of God" as recorded by Israel and New Breed.

Focus

⁶When we were utterly helpless, Christ came at just the right time and died for us sinners. ⁷Now, most people would not be willing to die for an upright person, though someone might perhaps be willing to die for a person who is especially good. ⁸But God showed his great love for us by sending Christ to die for us while we were still sinners. ⁹And since we have been made right in God's sight by the blood of Christ, he will certainly save us from God's condemnation. ¹⁰For since our friendship with God was restored by the death of his Son while we were still his enemies, we will certainly be saved through the life of his Son. ¹¹So now we can rejoice in our wonderful new relationship with God because our Lord Jesus Christ has made us friends of God.

(Romans 5:6-11)

And he said to them, "Go into all the world and proclaim the gospel to the whole creation."

(Mark 16:15 ESV)

Reflect

We have two pups at our house, Sam and Luna. They are both loving and precious. Sam has a laid-back, easygoing demeanor. Luna, on the other hand, is full of energy and even has a little bit of a mischievous nature from time to time. They both love to play a little game where we chase them around the yard. Sam, with his laid-back vibe, makes a lap and he's ready to be caught and cuddled. Luna, however, can go for a long time before she allows us to catch her and love on her. When she finally comes in for some love, I'm not sure if it's our company she wants or if she's just exhausted. Either way, it's nice when they come running to us.

As I pursue them, I sometimes think how God must see us like these pups in many ways. We wear ourselves out running around, darting here and there, evading pursuit only to find that once caught, the One chasing us was wanting to love on us the whole time. Some of us are like Sam, and we come to our senses pretty quickly and allow the One who pursues us to hold us and love on us. But for others, well, we have more of a Luna journey. We are a little slower to come to the reality that the God who pursues us does so with a love we will never fully understand.

What about you? Are you more like Sam or Luna? Why?

How quickly did you (and do you now) receive the love God so freely offers? Describe your response to God.

The meta-narrative (overall story) from Genesis to Revelation remains constant. God's love for His people is relentless. Although the settings and characters change with each generation, the theme of every book of the Bible is amazingly the same: God passionately pursues His people. In fact, He is so passionate in His pursuit that when it would appear we are beyond reach, He creates a new way for us to be reconciled to Him. He's just great like that! Though we may be rebellious and unfaithful, He is not. As we wander away from God's plan, He provides a way for us to be made whole, forgiven, and cleansed in order to live with Him eternally.

Read Romans 5:6-11 (page 196). In the space below, describe a person without Jesus and a person with Jesus. Use descriptions, adjectives, and phrases from these verses to help you.

Without Jesus   **With Jesus**

Take time today to remember your journey. Recall a few highs and lows of your spiritual life, noting the specific ways you now can see that God was pursuing you.

Highs:

Lows:

In our study, we have seen that from the very beginning, God pursues His people and provides for them even after sin enters the relationship. While enslaved in Egypt, God pursues them through an epic unfolding of miracles to deliver His people to a homeland designed especially for them. Even while in exile in Babylon, He sent prophets and leaders like Daniel, Nehemiah, and Ezra to guide and direct His people back to Him. Throughout the Old Testament God pursues His people even in their rebellion.

In the New Testament, God's pursuit of us is personified in Jesus. No greater love story can be offered than for God to send His Son to earth in human form to connect with us, teach us, sacrifice for us, and show us the way to heaven. No longer is animal sacrifice required. Jesus has become the sacrificial lamb who takes away the sins of the world (John 1:29). As we have seen, for all who put their faith and trust in Him, eternal life is promised.

This week, as we've seen, once we come to know Jesus, the pursuit is not over. Instead, we are invited to join God in pursuing others with His love and message. We are part of God's chosen family, and being part of the family means we inherit the work of the family business— sharing love through Christ.

> **Read Mark 16:15 (page 196).**
>
> **How will you join God in pursuing those far from Him? In the space below, write your game plan for sharing Christ. Think about who you will share with and how you will build those relationships so you can earn the right to share with them. Write down ways you can engage the individuals and show your care for them.**

We are part of God's chosen family, and being part of the family means we inherit the work of the family business— sharing love through Christ.

In elementary school, the kids in my neighborhood would often play hide-and-go-seek. Unlike most children, I hated that game. It made me anxious. Trying to find a great spot in which to hide and then nervously waiting to be discovered was stress that my little seven-year-old self just didn't want. I was actually relieved to be found, and it was even better if I was picked to be it and could avoid hiding in the first place. I'm not sure what that says about me, but somehow in my mind at least, the task of evading was stressful.

As I write this, Sam is cuddled up beside me while Luna is running her little heart out. I called out to both of them a few minutes ago. He came at once; she glanced my way but was still busy about her puppy activities. It's typical. She'll run around another minute or two and then head on over. There are times that I run around just like Luna. I wear myself out flitting from one thing to another. Like her, I stay busy, industrious, curious, not purposely trying to be distant. Left alone too long, like Luna, I can wander away from the watchful eye of my Master. But what I want to do is be more like Sam, responding immediately to the voice of the One who loves me. I want to fall into the arms of the One who pursues me. (Sam is already asleep now. Knowing that you're loved and cared for has that affect, doesn't it? It allows us to rest.)

Friend, you are loved and pursued by the God of the universe. My hope for you is that you can receive that truth in a new and fresh way today. You are desired, loved, and pursued by the One who knows you best. God's love for you is absolutely relentless! When the voices of this world crowd in, let this be the message you hear most clearly: the God of the universe passionately pursues you! You, my friend, are loved.

Prayer

Lord help me stay in step with You. Don't allow me to get in front of You or lag behind You. I surrender my will to Yours and want to live in harmony with Your Spirit. Help me receive Your love fully and then offer that same unconditional love to others. Thank You for pursuing me. Please give me a passion to pursue others in Your Name. Amen.

Video Viewer Guide
WEEK 6

Scriptures: Matthew 24:36, Mark 16:15, Matthew 28:19-20, John 1:43-51, Matthew 5:16, Colossians 4:5-6, Psalm 107:2, 1 Peter 3:15

Invite people to _____ and _____.

Become a _____-and-_____ believer.

Get _____.

Put together your _____ _____.

Pray for _____.

When you see someone hurting, _____.

Video Viewer Guide
ANSWERS

Week 1
give up

pursues

passionately loves

Week 2
sees

pursues

enough

Week 3
love / forgiveness

commands

committed

failures

Week 4
rescue mission

price / life

sacrifice / time

delights

Week 5
simple

available

deeds

Week 6
come / see

show / tell

ready

elevator story

opportunities

engage

Notes

Week 1

1. Jennifer Cowart, *Messy People: Life Lessons from Imperfect Biblical Heroes* (Nashville: Abingdon Press, 2018), 54–55.

Week 2

1. *Oxford English and Spanish Dictionary*, s.v. "bitterness," https://www.lexico.com/en/definition/bitterness.
2. Zev Farber, "How Is It Possible that Jacob Mistakes Leah for Rachel?" TheTorah.com, https://www.thetorah.com/article/how-is-it-possible-that-jacob-mistakes-leah-for-rachel.
3. Farber, "How Is It Possible that Jacob Mistakes Leah for Rachel?"
4. H. J. Howat, "Contrast between Elijah and Elisha," Bible Hub, https://biblehub.com/sermons/auth/howat/contrast_between_elijah_and_elisha.htm.

Week 4

1. Hayyim Schauss, "Ancient Jewish Marriage," My Jewish Learning, https://www.myjewishlearning.com/article/ancient-jewish-marriage/.
2. "What Were Common Marriage Customs in Bible Times?" Got Questions? https://www.gotquestions.org/marriage-customs.html.
3. "The Jewish Wedding Analogy," Bible Study Tools, https://www.biblestudytools.com/commentaries/revelation/related-topics/the-jewish-wedding-analogy.html.

Week 5

1. "Rabbi and Talmidim," That the World May Know, https://www.thattheworldmayknow.com/rabbi-and-talmidim.
2. Lois Tverberg, "Coverd in the Dust of Your Rabbi: An Urban Legend?" Our Rabbi Jesus, https://ourrabbijesus.com/covered-in-the-dust-of-your-rabbi-an-urban-legend/.

More Bible Studies from Jennifer Cowart

Learn from the fierce women of God who changed the world.
Fierce: Women of the Bible Who Changed the World

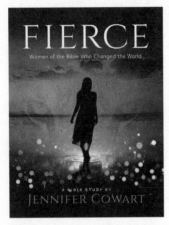

Participant Workbook | 9781501882906

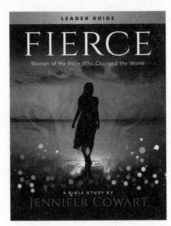

Leader Guide | 9781501882920

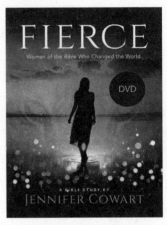

Video-DVD | 9781501882944

The word *fierce* is trendy. It is used to describe women who are extreme athletes, high-level executives, or supermodels. Women at the top of their game. But what about the rest of us? Can we be fierce? Absolutely! In fact, women like us have been changing the world for thousands of years—many who received little fanfare yet lived fiercely anyway. In this six-week study we will look at lesser-known female characters in the Bible and the ways they changed the world by living into God's calling, including:

- The midwives of Egypt (Shiphrah and Puah), who made hard decisions in the face of evil
- Deborah, who was an unlikely and powerful leader
- Naaman's slave girl, who bravely points others to God's healing power
- The Woman at the Well, who boldly repented and shared her faith
- Lois and Eunice, who parented with intentionality and effectiveness
- Dorcas, who showed kindness to those in need.

As we explore their lives, we will discover how we too can live into our callings, honor the Lord, and even change the world through our courage, faithfulness, and obedience.

Explore excerpts and video teaching samples at AbingdonWomen.com.

More Bible Studies from Jennifer Cowart

God can turn your messy life into a masterpiece.
Messy People: Life Lessons from Imperfect Biblical Heroes

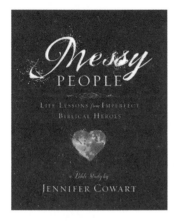 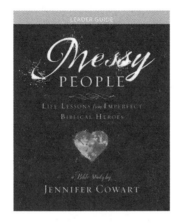 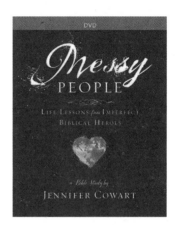

Participant Workbook | 9781501863127   Leader Guide | 9781501863141   Video-DVD | 9781501863165

Every life gets messy at times. Sometimes these messes are literal, like a house that would be easier to condemn than to clean. But sometimes they are intangible messes such as illness, conflict, depression, abuse, bankruptcy, divorce, and job loss. And these messes can be painful, hurting our hearts and our homes. But as we see in the Bible, God loves to use messy people!

In this six-week study, we will dig into the lives of biblical heroes who were messy people just like us but who were used by God in powerful ways.

Together we will examine the stories of five wonderful but messy people and one messy parable character:

- Rahab
- The Prodigal Son
- Josiah
- Mary
- David
- Daniel

From their stories, we will learn how God can use broken people, restore damaged hearts and relationships, give us power to handle our critics, and help us deal with the hard moments of life. Along the way we'll discover that we don't have to just endure messy lives but can actually learn to thrive with God's guidance and help. In the hands of God, our messes can become His masterpieces!

Explore excerpts and video teaching samples at AbingdonWomen.com.